The RAINBOW Pro

Robert O'Neill

BOOKS

Published by ZASTRUGI BOOKS
PO Box 2963
Brighton
East Sussex
BN1 6AW
UK

ISBN 1 902943 00 7

Designed by WILEMAN DESIGN
Cover and text illustrations by GARY ANDREWS

Originated in Singapore by SANG CHOY INTERNATIONAL PTE. LTD
Printed in Hong Kong by WING KING TONG CO. LTD

The author wishes to thank his friends and colleagues, Andy
Hewitson and Frank Steele, in Munich, for their valuable feedback
and suggestions.

The author and publisher would like to thank the manager of the
Cadillac Hotel, Venice, California, for permission to use the name
and location.

Apart from the obvious exceptions (San Francisco Police
Department, the Cadillac Hotel) the people and institutions
portrayed in the story element of this book are ficticious. Any
resemblance to people (living or dead) or institutions (current or
defunct) is an unfortunate coincidence.

TO THE USERS OF THIS BOOK

HOW MUCH ENGLISH DO I NEED?

Answer these three questions with 'yes' or 'no':

1   Look at the short READING text on page 8.
    Can you understand most of it?
2   Now read the CONVERSATION on page 12.
    Can you also understand most of it?
3   Can you understand questions 1 and 2 above?

If your answers to these questions is 'yes', you can use this book and learn a lot from it.

Units 1, 2 and 3 perhaps seem 'too easy' for your level. But these three units are really 'Revision' units. Perhaps you learned English a long time ago and have forgotten a lot. Sometimes, people forget even very 'simple' words. The texts and exercises in Units 1–3 will help you to remember what you have forgotten.

WHAT KIND OF ENGLISH WILL I LEARN?

■   International English

THE RAINBOW PROJECT is a story, and the story takes place in one of the most international cities in the world, San Francisco. People from all over the world live and work there. The characters in this book speak the kind of English that is used and understood all over the world. It is International English.

But what is International English? It is the kind of English a German businessperson uses when talking to a Greek businessperson, or a Japanese or a Polish engineer uses when talking to a Spanish engineer, or a young Italian student uses when talking to a Chinese student, or a French traveller uses when he or she is in Thailand, Kenya or Brazil.

■   Essential vocabulary and grammar for work, travel and general purposes

People who are learning English often say they are learning it for their jobs, or because they want to travel. Many of the people who say 'I need English for my job' don't have jobs yet. What they really mean is 'If I learn English, I will have a much better chance of getting a job'. When you read or listen to the English in this book, you are reading or listening to the kind of English people need when they work in an international company, or when they travel to other parts of the world.

WHAT KIND OF STORY IS IT? AND WHY USE A STORY TO TEACH ENGLISH?

■   A 'thriller' that is 'not only a thriller'

THE RAINBOW PROJECT is a 'thriller' – the kind of story that people often read for pleasure and which is usually about some sort of crime. This does not mean that THE RAINBOW PROJECT is 'just a story' or 'only for entertainment'. People often study English in the evenings or early in the morning. Sometimes, they are very tired. It is not enough if the English they are learning is useful, or is only the kind of English they need for work or travel. People learn far more easily if they are interested in the story they are reading and listening to.

■   You can read or listen to any part of the story even if you don't know – or have forgotten – other parts of the story

Perhaps you are studying English in an evening class, and perhaps you can't come to a lesson now and then. It doesn't matter. Look at any of the READING or CONVERSATION texts in the book – for example the READING texts on pages 16 and 60 and the CONVERSATION texts on pages 44 and 64. These are all different parts of the same story, but you can understand each READING or CONVERSATION text even if you haven't read any of the others.

■   A story for use in and outside the classroom

When people read or listen to an interesting story, they want to know the rest of the story. If you can't come to a lesson, you can still read or listen at home to the part of the story you missed in class. The more you read and listen to the story outside the class the more you will learn in the class.

■   A story about other people that helps you to talk about yourself

Look at Exercises 6A and 6B on page 22. Exercise 6A gives you information on one of the characters. In Exercise 6B, you complete questions that you use to get information from other people – questions which help you to talk about yourself.

You will find many exercises like this in THE RAINBOW PROJECT and many other exercises that encourage you to talk about yourselves, your life and your interests.

CONTENTS

KEY GRAMMAR	KEY VOCABULARY & PHRASES	THEMES & FUNCTIONS

Contents

Key Grammar	Key Vocabulary & Phrases	Themes & Functions

1 SERIOUS PROBLEMS

1 TALK ABOUT THE PICTURES

👥 **Work with someone else. Discuss these questions about the pictures.**

1 How do you think the man in the pictures feels?
2 Why does he feel this way? Think of different possible answers.
3 What kind of job do you think he does?
4 Where do you think he works?

2 🔊 READING

DAY 1 : MONDAY : 10.55 A.M. : FOSTER CITY

Tom Hellman comes from Boston, but he lives in San Francisco now. He works for Global Computer Systems. They are developing a new software program and he is the Project Manager.

Tom is married and has a daughter. His wife and daughter used to live with him in San Francisco, but they are back in Boston again.

Tom is sitting in his office in Foster City, near San Francisco. There are some very serious problems with the new software program and he is thinking about them. He's tired, depressed and very worried.

'I can't take it any more. There's only one thing I can do. It's the only way out,' he is thinking.

He looks at his watch. It is exactly ten fifty-five. Then he goes to the window and opens it. He is on the sixteenth floor. He looks down at the street below.

Look again at the questions in Exercise 1. Now that you have read the text, do you want to change any of your answers?

3 COMPREHENSION CHECK

A **Which of these sentences do you think are probably right? Which do you think are wrong? Read out something from the text in Exercise 2 that shows if it is right or wrong.**

EXAMPLE Tom is a happy man.
ANSWER No. According to the text, he is 'tired, depressed and very worried'.

1 Tom has a few problems but they aren't serious.
2 Perhaps he has a few family problems.
3 Tom has an important job with Global Computer Systems (GCS).
4 He has always lived in San Francisco.
5 'The only way out' in the text means 'the one door from the building to the street outside'.

B **Connect the two parts of the sentences (1–4; A–D).**

1 If you are *worried*,
2 If you are *depressed*,
3 If you are *tired*,
4 When you *develop* something,

A you want to sit down or lie down and perhaps go to sleep.
B you want to make it bigger or better.
C you are afraid that something bad or not very good is going to happen.
D you are sad, perhaps because the weather is very bad, or because something bad has happened in your life.

4 TALK ABOUT IT

Work with someone else. Choose a question you both want to answer. Then compare your answers.

■ Are you ever worried? If so, what are some of the things you worry about?

■ What do you think Tom is thinking about as he looks down from his office window on the sixteenth floor at the street below?

■ What do you think Tom can see from his office on the sixteenth floor?

5 FORM & MEANING

A **Discuss the meaning of the pairs of sentences. Is there an important difference in meaning? If so, what is that difference?**

▼ GRAMMAR 1A–B, p. 113
1 A Tom comes from Boston.
  B Tom is coming from Boston.

2 A Where do you come from?
  B Where are you coming from?

3 A Tom's wife lives in Boston.
  B Tom's wife is living in Boston.

▼ GRAMMAR 1C, p. 113
4 A Tom goes to the window and opens it.
  B Tom is going to the window . . . and now he's opening it.

B **Match the sentences above with the explanations below. (There are two sentences above for one of the explanations below.)**

A This sentence means that perhaps Tom is in a plane or on a train or in his car, and he is on his way from Boston to another place.
B This sentence tells us where Tom was born.
C This sentence means 'Where were you born?' or 'Where is your home?'
D This sentence means 'Where were you a few minutes ago?'
E This sentence could mean 'Tom's wife didn't live in Boston before, but that is where her home is now.'
F You can use this sentence if you are watching Tom in his office, and you can see Tom when he is in the middle of doing these things. Both actions are incomplete – not finished – when you say them.
G This sentence could be from a story, and in the story both actions are complete.

6 QUICK REVISION

A **Change the form of the words in brackets. Sometimes only one word is necessary. Sometimes two or even three words are necessary.**

EXAMPLES (*rain*) It often *rains* in Portland.
(*rain*) It *is raining* in Portland now.

▼ GRAMMAR 1A–B, p. 113

1 (*think*) Tom often ___ about his family.
2 (*think*) He ___ about his family now.
3 (*go*) His wife has a job. She usually ___ to work at eight o'clock.
4 (*go*) It is almost eight o'clock in Boston now. So probably she ___ to work now.
5 (*come*) Tom ___ to work three hours ago.
6 (*work*) In other words, Tom ___ in his office for three hours.
7 (*work*) He often ___ ten or more hours a day.
8 (*work*) Yesterday he ___ for eleven hours.
9 (*work*) What about you? How many hours a day ___ you usually ___?

B 👥 **Work with a partner. One of you completes the questions, the other answers them.**

1 ___ Tom married?
2 How ___ children does he have?
3 Where ___ his wife and daughter live now?
4 What ___ he thinking about?
5 What ___ you think he is going ___ do?

C 👥 **What about you? Complete these questions, too. Then ask your partner the complete question.**

1 (*live*) Where ___ you ___ now?
2 (*be*) Where ___ you born?
3 (*work*) ___ you ___ for a large company?
4 (*go*) What time ___ you usually ___ to work in the morning?
5 (*be*) ___ you married?
6 (*have*) ___ you ___ any children?
7 (*like*) What kinds of things ___ you ___ doing at the weekend?
8 (*do*) What ___ you ___ this weekend? Do you know?

7 SMALL BUT IMPORTANT WORDS

Use the words in the box to complete the sentences. Sometimes two different words are possible, but use only one.

he	him	His	his	she	her	they	them
their	it	that	which	what	who	there	

▼ GRAMMAR 11, p. 118 (THAT, WHO, WHICH)

Tom Hellman is from Boston but **1** ___ has been living in San Francisco for three years now. **2** ___ wife and daughter used to live **3** ___, too, but **4** ___ have gone back to Boston now. Tom works for an international company **5** ___ makes a wide range of computer software systems. The company is developing a new product called RAINBOW **6** ___ is very important for the company's future. Tom, **7** ___ is the Project Manager, has had some serious professional and personal problems lately. He doesn't know **8** ___ to do about **9** ___. Tom often thinks about **10** ___ wife. He loves **11** ___ and he knows that **12** ___ loves **13** ___, too. Sometimes he thinks that somehow they can find a way to solve **14** ___ problems. At other times he thinks **15** ___ isn't possible.

1 **Which sentence can you complete with *it* or *that*?**
2 **Which sentence or sentences can you complete with *which* or *that*?**

8 VOCABULARY PRACTICE

A The words on the left (1–9) are words or phrases for places, things or times. The words on the right (A–J) are words for actions – things that people do. Find the connections. Sometimes more than one connection is possible.

EXAMPLE   1   office / H   work

1	office	A	read
2	in the morning	B	go to
3	computer	C	get up
4	the radio	D	use
5	in the evening	E	travel by
6	bus or train	F	listen to
7	newspaper	G	relax
8	television	H	work
9	at lunchtime	I	watch
		J	eat

B 👤👤 Now talk to someone about the connections between you and the words and phrases in Exercise A. Make complete sentences about yourself.

EXAMPLE   office

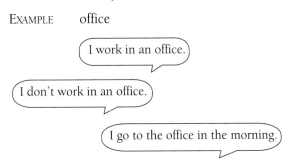

I work in an office.

I don't work in an office.

I go to the office in the morning.

C 👤👤 Think of questions you can ask your partners when they talk about the connections.

EXAMPLES

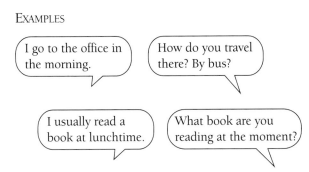

I go to the office in the morning.

How do you travel there? By bus?

I usually read a book at lunchtime.

What book are you reading at the moment?

9 🔊 LISTENING

This is Ros (Rosalind) Kovalski. She has a very interesting job. You'll learn more about her later. She is one of the people in the conversation you're going to hear. Listen to it. Then do the exercises below.

A True (T) or False (F)?

1 The man thinks that he knows Ros. ☐
2 Ros thinks she knows him, too. ☐
3 Ros says she is enjoying the party very much. ☐
4 The man says he isn't enjoying the party at all. ☐
5 The man's name is Miguel. ☐
6 He works for Global Computer Systems. ☐
7 Ros doesn't say who she works for. ☐

B Here is part (not all) of the conversation. What are the missing words?

MAN   **1** ___ to meet you, Ros.
KOVALSKI   **2** ___ here.
MAN   **3** ___ you **4** ___ the party?
KOVALSKI   No, not **5** ___.
MAN   No? Why **6** ___? I mean, what's wrong?
KOVALSKI   **7** ___ is wrong. Nothing at all. I just **8** ___ like parties very **9** ___. I never **10** ___ to **11** ___.
MAN   But you're at **12** ___ now.
KOVALSKI   I know.
MAN   Well, why **13** ___ you come to it if . . . if you don't like parties very much?
KOVALSKI   It's a little difficult to **14** ___. Let's just say I'm here **15** ___ of my job.

C Now answer these questions.

1 What are the four initials (letters) Ros mentions?
2 What exactly do the initials stand for?
3 What does Ros do?

2 HOTLINE

1 👥 TALK ABOUT IT

- Find out how many people in your class use computers.
- Find out who uses a computer to do the following things:
  - write letters
  - work with numbers
  - draw pictures
- Now think of some other things you can do with a computer.

2 CONVERSATION

A 🔊 Listen to the first part of the conversation.

DAY 1 : MONDAY : P.M. : GCS HOTLINE : LONDON

A MAN AND A WOMAN ARE TALKING ON THE PHONE. SHE WORKS FOR THE GCS 'HOTLINE' SERVICE. WHEN CUSTOMERS HAVE A PROBLEM WITH A GCS PRODUCT, THEY CAN CONTACT THE 'HOTLINE' SERVICE.

WOMAN How can I help, Mr Greenway?
MAN It's about your office management software.
WOMAN RAINBOW?
MAN Yes. We're testing the new version.
WOMAN You're testing RAINBOW 3? Is that right?
MAN Yes. The new version. RAINBOW 3.
WOMAN What did you use before?
MAN The old version of RAINBOW.
WOMAN Do you mean RAINBOW 2?
MAN Yes. Now we're using RAINBOW 3 . . . and we've had some problems.
WOMAN What kind of problems, sir?
MAN Serious problems.
WOMAN Could you describe a typical problem you've had with it, please?
MAN There are so many.
WOMAN How long have you been using RAINBOW 3?
MAN For about two weeks. It doesn't work nearly as well as RAINBOW 2 did.
WOMAN RAINBOW 3 is far more powerful than RAINBOW 2, Mr Greenway.

B 🔊 Now listen to the complete conversation, which includes a second part.

👥 **Then discuss these questions with your partners.**

1 Why does the woman say that RAINBOW 3 is far more 'powerful' than RAINBOW 2?
2 How many other people at Mr Greenway's company are using the new version of RAINBOW?
3 What do they all say about it?
4 Who is Mr Greenway going to talk to?
5 Why is he going to talk to this other person?

3 WORDS & MEANINGS

👥 Work with a partner. Connect the two parts of each sentence (1–7; A–G).

1 A *typical* problem is a problem that
2 A *serious* problem is a problem that
3 When you *describe* a problem,
4 When you find a *solution* to a problem, it
5 The *staff* of a company are the people that
6 A *version* of something is
7 When you give people more *training*,

A you say what happens when you have it.
B a copy of it that is different in some way.
C is no longer a problem.
D people are perhaps very worried about.
E work for that company.
F you often have or which other people often have.
G you teach them more things about something.

4 TALK ABOUT IT

👥 Choose one of the questions below. Talk about it with your partners.

- When was the last time you had a serious problem with a machine or something else you often use?

  Describe the problem and what you did about it.

- Describe the machines you use in your everyday life.

  What exactly do these machines do for you or help you to do?

- Talk about something people do with computers now and then describe how people did those same things thirty or forty years ago.

- You buy an expensive machine – perhaps a new computer, a television, or something else. It worked very well in the shop, but when you take it home it doesn't work very well.

  What is the best thing to do?

- You are late for a train. You put money in a ticket machine. The machine doesn't give you a ticket, but it takes your money. What do you do?

5 FORM & MEANING

A 👥 Explain the difference in meaning.

▼ GRAMMAR 2A, 3A, 4A, pp. 113–114
1 He used the software for about two weeks.
2 He has been using the software for about two weeks.
3 He used the software about two weeks ago.

Which sentence tells you:

A that he *is still using* the software?
B only *when* he *used* the software?
C *how long* he used the software, but not *when* he used it?

B Complete the sentences with these words:

for	since	in	on	at	ago

1 GCS has been in business ___ 1979.
2 Tom Hellman began working for GCS ___ 1996.
3 He was still living with his wife ___ that time.
4 His wife went back to Boston three months ___ .
5 In other words, she has been living in Boston ___ three months now.
6 Tom phoned her ___ Friday last week.
7 He has not spoken to her ___ then.
8 Their marriage has not been working well ___ some time.
9 Their daughter, Martha, was born nine years ___ .
10 The last time Tom saw her was three months ___ .

C 👥 Talk to your partners about two or three of the questions below. Then tell your teacher what you have learned about your partners.

- Describe something to your partners that you did for more than twenty minutes yesterday.

- Describe something that you have been doing for more than a year.

- Think of a photograph that someone took of you at least five years ago. In what way have you changed since then? Talk about how you looked then and how you look now.

6 VOCABULARY PRACTICE

A Connect the two parts of each sentence (1–8; A–H).

1 When you *use* something,
2 When you *need* something, you can't
3 When you *employ* someone,
4 When you *practise* something,
5 When you *discuss* something,
6 If something is *useful*,
7 If something is *useless*,
8 If someone gives you *practical* advice,

A you give that person a job.
B it doesn't help you at all to do anything.
C you work with it or do something with it.
D it helps you to do something.
E you do it often or regularly because you want to do it better.
F they say something that will help you.
G do a job without it.
H you talk about it with someone.

B Choose the best word from the box to complete each sentence.

| use need employ practise useful useless practical discuss |

1 How many people does this company ___?
2 You can't cut anything with this knife. It's absolutely ___.
3 This idea isn't going to work. It just isn't ___.
4 If you want to play the piano well, you have to ___ for hours and hours every day.
5 I live in a city with good buses and trains, so I don't really ___ a car.
6 A good English dictionary will be very ___ when you go to America.
7 Can I ___ your dictionary for a moment?
8 Come into my office, please. I want to ___ this report with you.

7 TALK ABOUT IT

Choose one of the questions below. Talk about it with your partners.

■ What is a practical way to use and practise your English if you don't live in an English-speaking country?

■ Describe three or four things you have bought recently.

  Which of the things is really useful? Why and how is it useful? Is there anything that isn't really useful?

■ Do people ever give you gifts or presents?

  Which gifts or presents have been useful to you? Have any been useless? What were the useful or useless gifts? Explain why they were useful or useless.

■ Some friends want to give you a present. It can be very expensive. Perhaps it isn't very useful, but it is something you want. Describe the gift you would like.

8))) PRONUNCIATION

A Say the four words in each group below. When does the sound of the underlined letter or letters change?

1 b<u>u</u>s b<u>u</u>siness c<u>u</u>stomer m<u>o</u>nth
2 bu<u>s</u> bu<u>s</u>iness hi<u>s</u> i<u>s</u>
3 discu<u>ss</u> bu<u>s</u> u<u>s</u>eful mu<u>s</u>t
4 <u>u</u>seful <u>u</u>seless b<u>u</u>s <u>u</u>ser
5 pr<u>o</u>gram g<u>o</u> kn<u>ow</u> kn<u>ow</u>ledge
6 d<u>o</u> pr<u>o</u>gram m<u>o</u>ment g<u>o</u>
7 h<u>o</u>tel h<u>o</u>t ph<u>o</u>ne g<u>o</u>
8 pr<u>o</u>duct pr<u>o</u>gram pr<u>o</u>blem pr<u>o</u>mise

B Now say all the words in Exercise A that have these sounds.

1 the sound of 'u' in b<u>u</u>s
2 the sound of 's' in bu<u>s</u>
3 the sound of 'u' in <u>u</u>seful
4 the sound of 'o' in g<u>o</u>
5 the sound of 'o' it h<u>o</u>t

9 TELEPHONE SKILLS

A 👥 **Robert Keller, who works at the GCS head office near San Francisco, is calling someone at the GCS branch office in London. Robert's part of the phone call (1–9) is in the correct order. The other part of the conversation (A–I) is not in the correct order.**

With a partner, read aloud the complete conversation. If you are Robert Keller, this will be easy. But your partner has to read aloud the responses in the correct order.

1 Good morning. Can I speak to Sue O'Brian, please?
2 Robert Keller.
3 No. Keller. K–E–L–L–E–R.
4 Thank you.
5 Very well, thanks, Sue. How are you?
6 I'm glad to hear that. Now, as you know, I'm coming to London tomorrow.
7 That's why I'm phoning now. I'm on European International Flight 569, arriving at nine-thirty tomorrow morning. Have you got that?
8 Exactly.
9 Thank you, Sue. I'm looking forward to seeing you again.

A Good. I'll be at the airport to meet you.
B Fine, thanks.
C Who's calling, please?
D Yes. Let me repeat it. EI five, six, nine. Arriving at nine-thirty a.m.
E One moment, please, Mr Keller. I'll put you through.
F Thank you, Robert. I'm looking forward to seeing you, too.
G Hello, Robert. How are you?
H Yes. But which flight will you be on? And when do you get here?
I Pardon? Did you say Kelly?

B 👥 **Now change roles. If you were Robert Keller before, your partner now reads aloud Robert's part and you read aloud the correct responses. Then do Exercise C below.**

C 👥 **Keep the same roles as in Exercise B above. But this time, the person reading aloud Robert Keller's part of the conversation tries to remember Robert's part without looking at the page.**

D 👥 **Change roles again. The partner that was Robert in Exercise A is Robert again, and tries to remember Robert's sentences without looking at the page.**

E **Now match the two parts of each sentence below.**

1 I'd like to speak
2 Hello, is
3 This is
4 I have the information
5 I'm arriving at
6 My flight number
7 Would you like me
8 I'm looking forward to

A Robert Keller in San Francisco.
B meeting you tomorrow.
C that Sue O'Brian?
D to repeat that information?
E to Sue O'Brian, please.
F nine-thirty tomorrow morning.
G you wanted.
H is EI569.

FLIGHT	ARRIVING FROM	ARRIVAL TIME	INFORMATION
BA173	ATHENS	08.30	LANDED
LH2323	MUNICH	08.35	
JL485	TOKYO	08.55	
EI569	SAN FRANCISCO	09.30	EXPECTED 10.20
BA2833	PARIS CHARLES DE GAULLE	09.40	DELAYED

FLIGHT ARRIVALS

3 JOB INTERVIEW

1 👥 TALK ABOUT IT

1 Describe what usually happens at a job interview.
2 Imagine you are going for a job interview at a very conservative bank.
   Describe the clothes you are going to wear.
3 Describe the typical things you think these people do every day:
   - A receptionist at a hotel.
   - A receptionist or secretary in a large, international company.
   - A driver for a security company or delivery service.

2 🔊 READING

DAY 1 : MONDAY : 10.45 A.M. : GCS HEADQUARTERS

The young man smiled at the receptionist.
  'Can you tell me where Mr Hellman's office is, please?'
  The receptionist smiled back.
  'Do you have an appointment with him?' she asked.
  'Yes. My name is Clarke – with an 'e' on the end.'
  'Please take a seat, Mr Clarke. I'll tell Mr Hellman that you're here.'
  Martin looked at his watch. It was ten forty-five. He was glad he was fifteen minutes early for the interview. All the books said that was very important.
  Five minutes later, two men in brown uniforms arrived. One of them was holding a small package in his hand. He showed it to the receptionist.
  'Fifteenth floor,' she said and pointed to the elevator.
  The two men went up together.
  'Nice job. One small package and two men deliver it,' Martin said. The receptionist laughed.
  When Martin looked at his watch again, it was ten fifty-five. A few minutes later, the phone rang. The receptionist answered it.
  'What? Are you sure?' she said in a very low voice.
  She looked shocked – very shocked. She stared at Martin. 'I'm afraid Mr Hellman can't see you,' she said in the same low voice.

  'Excuse me. I'm not sure I understand. You mean he can't interview me at all today?' Martin asked.
  The receptionist didn't seem to hear the question. 'There's been a terrible accident,' she said slowly.
  'Really? What happened?'
  'Mr Hellman fell from a window on the sixteenth floor a few minutes ago.'

3 COMPREHENSION CHECK

A 👥 **Work with a partner. Which of the explanations below do you think are right? Which are wrong?**

1 If you have an interview at eleven and you arrive at ten forty-five, you are *late* and not *early*.
2 If I say 'A doctor will be with you *soon*,' I mean 'A doctor will come in a few days or perhaps in a few weeks.'
3 If I *deliver* something, I take it to someone and give it to him or her.
4 When you *hear* something, perhaps you also listen to it, but perhaps you don't.
5 You can hear a *smile* but not see it.
6 When someone *laughs*, you can see it but not hear it.
7 If you say 'there's been an accident', you mean that something bad – or not very good – has happened.
8 If I say 'He didn't seem to hear,' I mean 'I think he heard.'

B **Look at the explanations in Exercise A again. Correct those that are wrong.**

EXAMPLE   EXPLANATION 1
POSSIBLE ANSWER   No. If you have an interview at eleven and you arrive at ten forty-five, you are *early* not *late*.

4 TALK ABOUT IT

👥 **Choose a question and discuss different possible answers with your partners.**

■ Why do books say it is important to arrive early for a job interview?

■ Why do you think Martin Clarke has read books on what to do at interviews?

■ What kind of information do you think the man with the package wanted, and what do you think he wanted to do?

5 FORM & MEANING

A 👥 **Which sentences sound more polite? What are the words that make them more polite, especially when you are speaking to someone you don't know?**

▼ GRAMMAR 5A–B, p. 115; 6A–C, p. 115; 19D, p.122

1 A   Can you tell me where Mr Hellman's office is?
  B   Tell me where Mr Hellman's office is.

2 A   Excuse me. Do you know what time it is?
  B   What time is it?

3 A   What are you doing here?
  B   Do you mind if I ask what you're doing here?

4 A   I want to use your phone.
  B   Do you mind if I use your phone?

5 A   How does this machine work?
  B   Could you tell me how this machine works?

B **Change the direct questions ('Where is the station?') into indirect questions that begin with 'Can you tell me . . . ?'**

EXAMPLE   Where is the station?
           Can you tell me where the station is?

1 Where is the elevator?
2 Where is Mr Hellman's office?
3 Where is he now?
4 What are indirect questions?
5 Why are they called 'indirect'?
6 Why are they more polite than direct questions?

C **Now use the words in brackets ( ) after each direct question to change that question into an indirect question.**

EXAMPLE   Who is that man? (*Do you know*)
           Do you know who that man is?

1 Who is that man in the brown uniform? (*Do you know*)
2 Where is he going? (*Did you ask him*)
3 Who is the other man? (*Can you tell me*)
4 What do they want? (*Please ask them*)
5 Who is the package for? (*Did they say*)
6 What is in the package? (*Have you any idea*)
7 What did you just say? (*Could you please repeat*)
8 Was this a useful exercise? (*Did you think*)

6 VOCABULARY REVISION

A **Match the words with the numbers.**

ear   mouth   hand   eye   nose

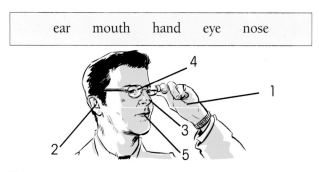

B **How many connections can you find between the five words on the left and the ten words on the right?**

EAR	see
	hear
MOUTH	look
	smell
HAND	speak
	carry
EYE	watch
	talk
NOSE	listen
	hold

C 🗨 **Work with a partner. Match sentences 1–8 with meanings A–H.**

1 Please *carry* this.
2 Please *hold* this.
3 Your problem is that you *speak* too much.
4 Your problem is that you *talk* too much.
5 I can't *hear* you any more.
6 I can't *listen* to you any more.
7 I can't *watch* this any more.
8 I can't *look* at this any more

A Take this in your hand. Don't do anything with it and don't drop it.
B You have a problem with your voice because you use it too often.
C I have no more time for this conversation.
D Take this in your hand and walk with it.
E Your problem is that you say things when it is better to say nothing.
F Perhaps there is something wrong with my ears or with the telephone.
G This film is terrible.
H This small computer screen is hurting my eyes.

7 📢 PRONUNCIATION

Say the pairs of words. Is the sound of the underlined letters the same or different?

1	<u>ea</u>r	<u>h</u>ear
2	<u>ea</u>r	h<u>ere</u>
3	h<u>ear</u>	h<u>ear</u>d
4	n<u>o</u>se	kn<u>ow</u>s
5	s<u>ee</u>	sp<u>ea</u>k
6	w<u>a</u>tch	t<u>a</u>lk
7	th<u>u</u>mb	s<u>o</u>me
8	h<u>ea</u>d	h<u>ea</u>r
9	h<u>ea</u>d	s<u>ai</u>d
10	elb<u>ow</u>	n<u>ow</u>

8 IS IT POLITE?

A 🗨 **Read the conversation aloud with a partner. Then discuss what person B says. Is she always polite? Make any changes you think are necessary.**

A Is that Global Computer Systems?
B Yes. What do you want?
A I'd like to speak to Mr Bondy.
B Mr Bondy isn't here. Leave a message if you want.
A Just tell him that I phoned. My name is Kovalski.
B Spell it.
A K–O–V–A–L–S–K–I.
B You didn't say the last letter clearly. Say it again.
A I.
B Y?
A No, 'I', as in India.
B Is that all?
A Yes, that's all.
B Goodbye.

B **Say these things in a more polite way.**

1 I'm busy at the moment.
2 Come back in a few minutes.
3 What did you say? Repeat it.
4 I can't hear you. Speak louder.
5 Tell me how to start this machine.
6 Say your name again.
7 I haven't got the information you want.
8 I can't come tomorrow evening. Change our appointment to another day.

9 TELEPHONE SKILLS

A Two people, A and B, are talking on the phone. Some words (1–10) are missing from their conversation. What do you think those missing words are?

A Global Computer Systems. Good morning.

B Sorry, I **1**___ hear that. Is that GCS?

A Yes, this is Global Computer Systems. How can I **2**___ you?

B I'd like to speak to Mr Bondy, the Technical Director, please.

A I'm **3**___ Mr Bondy isn't available at the moment. Would you like to **4**___ a message?

B No. Just **5**___ him that I called. My name is Kovalski.

A I'm **6**___ but I don't think I **7**___ that correctly. Could you spell your name, please?

B K–O–V–A–L–S–K–I.

A Pardon? What was the last letter? Did you **8**___ 'Y', as in Yankee?

B No. 'I', as in India.

A I see. Is that all, Ms Kovalski?

B Yes, that's all.

A Thank you, Ms Kovalski. Have a nice **9**___.

B Thanks. The **10**___ to you.

B Here are six of the missing words in Exercise A. But where do they belong?

sorry afraid same didn't heard tell

C ✪ Compare the complete conversation in Exercise A with the conversation in Exercise 8A on page 18. What are the most important changes?

10 ◖)) LISTENING

You are going to hear a very different kind of conversation from the one in Exercise 9. Two men are speaking. Listen to the conversation. Then do the exercises below.

A ✪ How many of these questions can you and your partner answer?

1 What time do you think it was when this conversation took place?

2 Where do you think the two men were at the time of this conversation?

3 Why was one of them angry?

4 What did the other man want to talk about?

5 Why do you think he wanted to talk about it?

6 One of the two men said 'You took the money. I didn't.' What money do you think he is talking about?

7 One of the two men said 'So do it! Or you really will have a problem'. There are many different possible meanings here. Think of just one.

8 There is a connection between this conversation and Unit 1 (Exercise 2). Explain what you think the connection is or could be.

B Study the words and examples (1–3). Connect each word with its meaning (A–C).

1 ADVISE   My doctor *advised* me to stop smoking.

2 ORDER   The policeman *ordered* the criminal to throw down his gun.

3 THREATEN   The criminal *threatened* to kill me if I didn't give him all my money.

A . . . to do what a general in the army does when he tells soldiers 'Shoot', 'Kill', etc.

B . . . what parents sometimes do when they say that something very bad will happen if a child doesn't listen.

C . . . what you do when you tell a friend what you think he or she should do.

C Listen to the conversation again. One of the men does two of the things in Exercise B. What are they? Which of the three things does he not do?

4 A CHANGE OF PLAN

1 👥 TALK ABOUT THE PICTURES

1 Which man do you think is the other man's boss?
2 What is one man giving the other man?
3 What do you think the other man is going to do with it?

2 CONVERSATION

A 🔊 Listen to the first part of the conversation.

DAY 2 : TUESDAY : LATE MORNING : GCS HEADQUARTERS

ROBERT KELLER AND LARRY KNOWLES ARE TALKING IN LARRY'S OFFICE.

LARRY   I suppose you've heard the . . . uh . . . the news.
ROBERT   Yes, I have. It's terrible. I can't believe it. Was it an accident?
LARRY   No. He committed suicide. He left a note on his desk.
ROBERT   What did he say in it?
LARRY   'Nobody will understand why I have done this, but it's the only way out. Please tell my wife and daughter that I love them very much.' Those were his exact words.
ROBERT   How could he do such a thing?
LARRY   His marriage wasn't working very well. And then there were all these problems with RAINBOW. That's really what I wanted to talk to you about, Robert. How can we save the project? It's been an awful headache from the very beginning.
ROBERT   But I've never been very involved in the project.
LARRY   I know you haven't. That's why I want your opinion.
ROBERT   But Ed Bondy is the Technical Director. What does he think?
LARRY   Ed is too involved in the project. He can't be objective. But you can.
ROBERT   But I don't know the facts.
LARRY   I know you don't. That's why I'd like you to read this report. I've underlined all the most important information.

B 🔊 Now listen to the complete conversation, which includes a second part.

👥 Then discuss these questions with your partners.

1 What do you think this conversation has to do with Tom Hellman in Unit 1? (*See page 8*)
2 What happened to Tom? What do the two men in the conversation think he did?
3 Where is one of the men going in a few minutes?
4 One of the men says 'I'd like you to change those arrangements'. Which arrangements?
5 Why does he want the other man to change his arrangements?

3 WORDS & MEANINGS

A Which explanations below do you agree with? Correct the explanations you don't agree with.

1 If you *suppose* something is true, you aren't certain it is true, but you think it is probably true.
2 *Accidents* are usually good things that people plan before they have them.
3 When people *commit suicide*, they kill other people and not themselves.
4 When people *leave a note*, they always say it and never write it.
5 If you are *involved* in a project, you do some of the work on that project.
6 When you give an *opinion*, you say only what you know is true and not what you think is true.
7 If you talk only about personal feelings and not what you think is true, it is an *objective* opinion.

B Complete the sentences below.

1 I didn't want this to happen. It was an ___.
2 If this story is in all the newspapers, I ___ it's probably true.
3 Don't talk about your feelings. Try to give me an opinion that is as ___ as possible.
4 How long has he been ___ in this kind of work?
5 A woman came to see you when you weren't here. She left a ___ for you. Here it is.
6 A few years ago I was terribly depressed. I even thought of committing ___.
7 I'm not interested in what the police think. Give me your own ___.

4 ◗)) PRONUNCIATION

A Listen to the three words alone and then in sentences. Notice how the sound changes.

do   What *do* you think?
does   What *does* Ed Bondy think?
did   What *did* he say?

B Now pronounce these sentences. Then listen to them.

What do you know about this?
What does Ed know about it?
What did he do about it?

5 FORM & MEANING

A 👥 Explain the difference in meaning between the two sentences in each pair.

▼ GRAMMAR 13A–B, p. 119

1 A   Robert's boss wants to read the report.
  B   Robert's boss wants him to read the report.

2 A   I'd like you to read this note.
  B   I'd like to read this note to you.

3 A   The teacher wants us to explain the difference.
  B   The teacher wants to explain the difference to us.

4 A   The boss would like to be at the meeting on Sunday.
  B   The boss would like you to be at the meeting on Sunday.

B 👥 Read aloud the eight sentences in Exercise A again. Then explain to your partners who is going to do what in each sentence.

EXAMPLE   1 A   Robert's boss wants to read the report.

ANSWER   Robert's boss and not Robert is going to read the report.

C Complete the second sentence in each pair so that it is more polite than the first sentence.

EXAMPLE   Say that again.
          Could *you say* that again, please?

1 Read this!
  I'd like ___ ___ ___ this.
2 Come to our party tomorrow!
  We'd like ___ ___ ___ to our party tomorrow.
3 Close that window!
  Would ___ ___ that window, please?
4 Repeat what you've just said.
  Could ___ ___ what you've just said, please?
5 Finish this job before five o'clock.
  Do you think ___ ___ ___ this job before five o'clock?
6 Come tomorrow.
  Would it be possible for ___ ___ ___ tomorrow?

6 READ & TALK ABOUT IT

A Read about Robert Keller.

Robert was born in Strasbourg, in France. His mother is American and his father is French. Robert grew up and went to school in Strasbourg. When he was eighteen, he went to Paris, where he studied at Nanterre University. When he was twenty-three, he got a job with Global Computer Systems, an American company. He has been working for GCS for six years and now lives in a small apartment in San Francisco.

Robert is single and has no children. He is interested in opera, modern art, baseball and boats. He has a small sportscar and a small boat, too. He speaks French, English and Spanish. He is now learning Japanese, but doesn't speak or read it very well.

B How many differences are there between your partners and Robert Keller? Begin by completing the questions below. Then ask your partners the completed questions.

1 ___ you born in Strasbourg?
2 ___ your mother American?
3 Where ___ you grow up?
4 ___ you go to school there, too?
5 ___ you work for an American company?
6 ___ you have a boat?

C Now use the information about Robert in Exercise A to ask your partners more questions. Find out if they are interested in the same things Robert is, how many languages they speak, and so on.

D Now talk to a new partner. Tell your new partner what you know about your old partner.

EXAMPLES

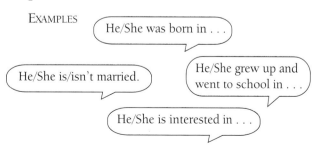

He/She was born in . . .

He/She is/isn't married.

He/She grew up and went to school in . . .

He/She is interested in . . .

7 VOCABULARY PRACTICE

A Connect the two parts of each question.

1 How old were you when you
2 At what age did you start
3 At what age do people usually
4 How old were you when
5 Do many people

A get their first jobs?
B you started school?
C began speaking?
D have children before they are eighteen?
E walking?

Here is a possible answer to one of the questions above. Which question do you think it is?

'That's difficult to say. Some people do it when they are eighteen or even younger. Others do it later. And some people never do it at all.'

B Now ask your partners the complete questions in Exercise A.

C Here are some more important 'events' in people's lives (1–6). Work with a partner and match an event with a description (A–F).

1 get married
2 retire
3 learn to drive
4 fall in love
5 get divorced
6 become a grandmother or grandfather

A This happens when your children have their own children.
B People often do this at sixty-five, or even earlier, when they stop working.
C Married people do this when they don't want to be married any more.
D This can happen at any age, but it is usually better to do it when you are young and your eyesight is good.
E This is the way people feel when they think they can't live without someone else.
F This is what they often do when they want to stay together for the rest of their lives.

8 TALKING ABOUT TRAVEL

A Say the best way to complete each question.

1 How often do you travel ___ air?
   A in **B** by **C** on

2 Do you enjoy ___?
   A travelling **B** the travel **C** to travel

3 How ___ usually travel?
   A you do **B** are you **C** do you

4 What's the longest journey you've ever ___?
   A taking **B** taken **C** took

5 How long did it ___ to get there?
   A you need **B** need you **C** take you

6 How ___ get there?
   A you **B** are you **C** did you

7 How do you usually pass the time ___ a long journey?
   A on **B** for **C** in

B Here are some possible answers to the questions in Exercise A. Match the answers with the questions.

A All sorts of ways. It depends on where I'm going. Sometimes I fly. Sometimes I take a train or a bus.

B In all sorts of ways. Sometimes I read. Sometimes I talk to someone. And sometimes I sleep.

C Sometimes I do. Sometimes I don't. Again, it depends.

D Sydney to Paris via Tokyo.

E I flew, of course.

F I can't remember, but I think at least twenty-four hours. Perhaps longer.

G Many times a year.

C Now ask your partners the completed questions in Exercise A.

D Now talk to a new partner. Tell your new partner what you learned about your old partner.

EXAMPLE
> I talked to (name). The longest journey he/she has ever taken was to . . . It took him/her (time) to get there.

9 LISTENING

A You are going to hear Robert Keller talking. Someone has asked him five of the following questions. You will hear only Robert's answers, not the questions. Listen and find out which five questions he was asked.

1 How do you prefer to travel?
2 How do you pass the time on a long journey?
3 Do you fly very often?
4 How do you usually get to work?
5 What's the longest journey you've ever taken?
6 Do you enjoy travelling by boat?
7 How long does it take you to get to work?

B Listen to each answer again. Then complete the sentences below.

A Robert is talking about a journey he **1** ___ two years **2** ___. First he **3** ___ to Japan and then to **4** ___. And from there he flew to **5** ___ and finally back to San Francisco.

B Robert is talking about **1** ___ he prefers to travel just around the Bay in his small **2** ___. Whenever possible he goes **3** ___ at weekends.

C Robert is talking about how **1** ___ it takes him to **2** ___ to work. He says this can **3** ___ on the **4** ___. That is why he often **5** ___ home very early.

D Robert says that he **1** ___ there. It's the only possible **2** ___ because there are no **3** ___ or **4** ___ that go there.

E Robert says that he **1** ___ enjoy **2** ___ at all, even though he travels Business or First **3** ___. He does it because he **4** ___ to, not because he **5** ___ to.

5 A DARK TUNNEL

1 👥 TALK ABOUT THE PICTURES

1 Look at picture 1. Where do you think the man is?
2 What is he doing there?
3 Why is he there?
4 Now look at picture 3. Where is the man now?
5 What do you think he has done in the last two or three hours?

2))) READING

DAY 2 : TUESDAY : EARLY AFTERNOON : SAN FRANCISCO AIRPORT

'Window or aisle?' the attendant at the airport check-in asked.

'Window, please,' Robert answered.

'I'm afraid there will be a slight delay this evening,' the attendant told him.

'A slight delay? How long exactly?'

'No more than half an hour, we hope.'

Robert walked into the Business Class lounge, and took a seat near the window. The sun was just setting – one of the most beautiful moments in the day in California. However, this evening he was not really in the mood to watch it.

He opened his briefcase and took out a document marked 'RAINBOW. Strictly Confidential'. Two sentences were underlined on page two.

We have recently learned that DS is developing a software project that is very similar to RAINBOW. According to our sources, it will be released within two months.

Robert found the two sentences difficult to believe. 'DS' – or 'Daring Solutions' was a very small company that had only one successful product – a program that calculated income and sales tax automatically. However, if those sentences were true – and if people found the DS program easier to use than RAINBOW – it would be very bad news indeed for GCS.

Two hours later, Robert had boarded the plane and was in the air, flying east. The sun had set. He was tired but he found it difficult to sleep. He had the feeling that he was flying into a dark tunnel.

Look again at the questions in Exercise 1. Now that you have read the text, do you want to change any of your answers?

3 COMPREHENSION CHECK

A   Which explanations below do you agree with? Correct the explanations you don't agree with.

1   If you have an *aisle* seat, it is very difficult for you to stand up and walk around in a plane.
2   The sun *sets* in the morning and *rises* in the evening.
3   If you are *in the mood* to do something, you want to do it or are ready to do it at that time.
4   'To board' a plane means 'to get off' the plane.
5   If you have the *feeling* that you are flying into a dark tunnel, you are really flying into a dark tunnel.

B   Look at the three pictures on the opposite page again. Say the number of the picture or pictures that go with each sentence below.

1   Two hours later, Robert had boarded the plane and was in the air.
2   He opened his briefcase and took out a document . . .
3   He was tired but he found it difficult to sleep.

C   ☻☺ Read aloud other sentences from the text that you think go with one or more of the pictures. Don't say which picture or pictures. Your partner has to say the picture numbers.

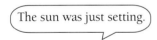 The sun was just setting.   Picture one.

4 TALK ABOUT IT

☻☺ Choose one or more questions and discuss possible answers with a partner.

■   What are at least three different things that usually happen at an airport check-in?

■   What do you think was the most important information that Robert got at the check-in?

■   Why do you think Robert found the underlined information in the report difficult to believe?

■   What exactly 'would be very bad news indeed for GCS' – and why would it be 'bad news'?

■   Why do you think Robert 'had the feeling that he was flying into a dark tunnel'?

5 FORM & MEANING

A   ☻☺ Explain the difference in meaning between the two sentences in each pair.

▼ GRAMMAR 2A–D, p. 113

1 A   When the plane took off, the sun was setting.
  B   When the plane took off, the sun had set.

■   **Which sentence means 'it was no longer possible to see the sun'?**

2 A   What was Robert doing when he heard about the delay?
  B   What did Robert do when he heard about the delay?

■   **Which of the two questions could you answer in the following way?**

   'He sat down and waited for more information.'

B   What is the best way to complete the sentences?

1   After the plane took off, Robert ___ the report from beginning to end again.
    A was reading   B read   C has read

2   Sue O'Brian woke up early that morning in London and looked out of the window. It ___.
    A was raining   B rained   C has been raining

3   By the time the plane landed in London, Robert ___ the report twice.
    A was reading   B had read   C read

4   Sue ___ for Robert when he walked out of the ARRIVALS door.
    A waited   B was waiting   C had waited

5   Sue said 'Hello' and then ___ Robert to his hotel in a taxi.
    A took   B was taking   C had taken

6   Linda Shawcross ___ in her office that morning when the telephone rang.
    A worked   B was working   C has worked

7   When the telephone rang, Linda ___ it.
    A answered   B was answering   C has answered

8   Linda did not know Robert. She ___ him before.
    A didn't meet   B hasn't met   C hadn't met

6 VOCABULARY PRACTICE

A Match the words (1–11) with their opposites (A–K).

1	delayed	A	considerable
2	cancel	B	dark
3	east	C	south
4	wake up	D	aisle
5	slight	E	confirm
6	sunrise	F	land
7	dawn	G	on time
8	take off	H	dusk
9	north	I	west
10	bright	J	fall asleep
11	window	K	sunset

B Now match words 1–9 with the explanations (A–I).

1	sunrise	A	what you see in the west on a clear day just before the sun disappears
2	morning		
3	noon		
4	afternoon	B	the time when the sun is going down and it is beginning to get dark
5	sunset		
6	dusk		
7	evening	C	immediately after 11.59 at night
8	night	D	immediately after 11.59 in the morning
9	midnight		
		E	the time in the day between 12 noon and when the sun goes down
		F	the early part of the day
		G	what you see in the east when the sun comes up
		H	the time after the sun goes down until most people go to bed
		I	the dark part of each day – also the time when most people sleep

7 TALK ABOUT IT

Suppose someone said the following things to you. Exactly *when* do you think the person speaking to you has in mind?

1 Let's see, it's Monday now. Could we postpone our meeting until sometime later this week?
2 Could I see you sometime later this afternoon?
3 Let's get together just before lunch-time.
4 I'll phone you around dinner-time. Is that OK?
5 Will you report back to me on this early this afternoon?
6 I got a call in the middle of the night last week.
7 I'd like to discuss this with you early tomorrow morning. What's the earliest time that's convenient for you?
8 The meeting took place early in the afternoon.
9 We would prefer the meeting to take place early next month.

8))) PRONUNCIATION

A Underline the part of the following words that is stressed.

EXAMPLE <u>sun</u>set

delay   confirm   product   believe   program
cancel   release   income   postpone   design
morning   afternoon   evening   midnight

B Now say each pair of words below. Is the sound of the underlined letters the same or different?

EXAMPLE n<u>oo</u>n   d<u>o</u>
ANSWER   The same.

1	d<u>o</u>	g<u>o</u>
2	d<u>one</u>	g<u>one</u>
3	d<u>one</u>	s<u>un</u>
4	g<u>one</u>	ph<u>one</u>
5	n<u>oo</u>n	s<u>oo</u>n
6	s<u>oo</u>n	f<u>oo</u>t
7	f<u>oo</u>d	g<u>oo</u>d
8	g<u>oo</u>d	w<u>ou</u>ld
9	w<u>ou</u>ld	w<u>oo</u>d
10	a<u>isle</u>	sm<u>ile</u>

9 🔊 LISTENING

A You are going to hear three different extracts. Stop the recording each time you hear the 'signal'. Then choose the answer that you think is correct (A, B or C) for each question below.

EXTRACT 1
Who do you think Robert Keller is phoning?

A   His secretary.
B   Someone who works in the London office of GCS (Global Computer Systems, the same company that Robert works for).
C   Someone in the airport information department.

EXTRACT 2
When do you think you would hear someone saying this?

A   Before you get on the plane.
B   Before the plane has taken off.
C   Just after the plane has taken off.

EXTRACT 3
When do you think this announcement was made?

A   Just before the plane took off.
B   Just before the plane landed.
C   Early in the flight.

B Listen to the three extracts a second time. Then answer these questions.

EXTRACT 1
1   What do you think Robert was looking for when he said 'Just a moment. It's here, I think'?
2   Imagine you are the person Robert is speaking to. Explain what you would say in the fax that Robert asks you to send.

EXTRACT 2
1   What is the purpose of this announcement?
2   What do you think is the most important information you have just heard?

EXTRACT 3
1   How long had the plane been in the air when this announcement was made?
2   What season or time of the year do you think it was in England when the announcement was made?

10 TAKING MESSAGES

A Here are some of the things Robert said to his secretary. Match the two parts of each sentence.

1   I've just been told there's going
2   I'd like you to fax
3   Just tell her that the plane
4   Yes. Give her my flight number so that she
5   Just a moment . . . It's EI 569. That's 'E'
6   Yes, that's all. Thanks for

A   your help, Margaret.
B   can find out from flight information when it arrives.
C   to be a delay.
D   Sue O' Brian in London.
E   may be late.
F   for Elisabeth and 'I' for India.

B And here are the secretary's answers. Match the answers with the sentences in Exercise A.

A   All right. I'll do that. What's the message you want me to give her?　[2D]
B   Not at all. Have a nice flight.　☐
C   Anything else?　☐
D   All right, I'll do that, too. Is that all?　☐
E   I'm sorry to hear that. What can I do to help?　☐
F   I don't think I have it. Can you give it to me?　☐

C 👥 Read aloud the complete conversation. One of you is Robert. The other is the secretary.

D The text below is the fax that Robert's secretary sent to London. However, in some lines (not all) there is one word that should not be there. Underline that word.

Robert Keller has phoned me a few minutes ago and asked me to tell to you that his plane may be delayed. Please check with airport information for the correct arrival time before you will go to the airport. His flight number is EI 569.

6 IS THIS A GRAMMAR LESSON?

1 👥 TALK ABOUT IT

1 Explain to your partners the difference between 'suicide' and 'murder'.
2 How is it possible for someone to murder someone else and arrange things so that other people think it was 'suicide'?

2 CONVERSATION

A 🔊 **Listen to the first part of the conversation.**

DAY 2 : TUESDAY : EVENING : SAN FRANCISCO POLICE DEPARTMENT

TWO DETECTIVES, SERGEANT ROS KOVALSKI AND HER BOSS, LIEUTENANT STEVE FERRANTE, ARE TALKING.

KOVALSKI The Hellman case isn't as simple as it seems.

FERRANTE It seems pretty simple to me. He had family problems and he was under a lot of pressure at work, as well. So he took a short walk and then a very long jump. Happens all the time.

KOVALSKI Perhaps he didn't jump. Perhaps he was pushed.

FERRANTE Pushed? What do you mean? People who are pushed out of a window don't leave suicide notes behind.

KOVALSKI Yes, but the note was printed.

FERRANTE Yeah. Hellman wrote the note on his computer. So what?

KOVALSKI No. The note was written on Hellman's computer.

FERRANTE Is this a grammar lesson, Ros? I say 'he wrote the note on his computer' and you say 'it was written on his computer'. What's the difference?

KOVALSKI How many suicide cases have you had since you became a policeman, Steve?

FERRANTE About a hundred, I suppose. Why?

KOVALSKI How often were notes left behind?

FERRANTE In at least half of the cases. Why?

KOVALSKI How many notes were printed?

FERRANTE None. All of them were hand-written. But this guy Hellman was a computer freak.

B 🔊 **Now listen to the complete conversation, which includes a second part.**

👥 **Then discuss these questions with your partners.**

1 Why does Steve think the case is simple?
2 Why does Ros think it isn't as simple as it seems?
3 Why does she think it is strange that Hellman had more than $400 in his pocket when he died?

3 COMPREHENSION CHECK

Which explanations do you agree with? Correct the explanations you don't agree with.

1 The 'case' Ros and Steve are talking about is something you can put clothes or documents in.
2 A 'very short walk and a very long jump' here means 'something very good athletes do in the Olympic Games'.
3 If we say 'the note was printed', we don't say who printed the note.
4 When something happens 'in at least half of the cases' it means it happens fifty per cent or more of the time.
5 'A computer freak' is someone who isn't interested in computers and never uses them.
6 When you wipe a computer keyboard clean, no dirt, fingerprints, etc. are left.

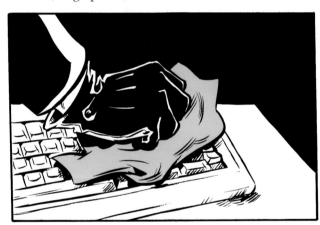

4 TALK ABOUT IT

Choose any question below and talk about it with your partners.

■ People who murder other people usually have a 'motive' – or a reason for killing someone. What are three common motives for murder?

■ If someone murdered Tom Hellman, what was a possible motive?

■ Do you remember reading about any 'murder cases' in the newspapers? If so, tell someone else everything you remember about the case.

■ Newspapers have different 'sections' (Sports, Business, International News, National News, etc.). Which section or sections do you usually read? Which sections do you usually not read?

5 FORM & MEANING

A 🖤 **Study the three pairs of sentences. In which pair or pairs is there an important difference in meaning? Which pair or pairs mean more or less the same thing?**

▼ GRAMMAR 7A–B, p. 116

1 A Perhaps Hellman pushed someone out of the window.
  B Perhaps Hellman was pushed out of the window by someone.

2 A Perhaps someone pushed him out of the window.
  B Perhaps he was pushed out of the window.

3 A Perhaps he didn't write the suicide note. Someone else did.
  B Perhaps the suicide note wasn't written by him, but by someone else.

Read aloud the sentence or sentences with the meanings below.

■ Hellman fell out of the window, but he didn't jump.

■ It is possible that someone else – not Hellman – wrote the suicide note.

B Complete each sentence below with the correct form of the verb in brackets ( ).

EXAMPLE (write) The suicide note _was written_ by someone else, not by Hellman.

1 (push) Hellman is dead now because he ___ out of a window.

2 (push) Hellman is dead now because someone ___ him out of a window.

3 (kill) Every year, thousands of people ___ in accidents.

4 (kill) Do you know how many people ___ in accidents last year?

5 (rob) Yesterday three men ___ a big bank in San Francisco.

6 (steal) They ___ over two million dollars.

7 (rob/steal) Yesterday a big bank in San Francisco ___ and over two million dollars ___.

6 VOCABULARY PRACTICE

A Match words 1–8 with definitions A–H.

1 kill   5 murderer
2 murder   6 thief
3 steal   7 robber
4 rob   8 suicide

A   To take something that is not yours.

B   To finish another person's life, sometimes accidentally.

C   To plan to kill someone and then to kill that person.

D   A person who takes something (perhaps a wallet or something small) that is not his or hers.

E   What you do to a person or a place when you take something that is not yours from that person or place.

F   A person who plans to kill someone and then does it.

G   What people commit when they kill themselves.

H   A person, usually but not always, who has a knife or a gun, and who steals from a person, a bank or some other place.

B 👥 Work with a partner. Say the word you think is the right word to complete each sentence.

1   If someone pushed Tom Hellman out of a window, this is not a case of ___.
    A murder   B suicide

2   If someone pushed him out of a window, this is a case of ___.
    A murder   B suicide

3   Nothing is missing from his office. In other words, nothing was ___.
    A stolen   B robbed

4   Nothing was missing from his pockets, either, so Tom Hellman wasn't ___.
    A stolen   B robbed

5   I think someone planned everything very carefully. But who? Who is the ___?
    A murder   B murderer

6   And why did that person ___ Hellman?
    A murder   B murderer

7 WORD PARTNERS

A Write the number of the word below (1 or 2) that can be used with each word or phrase A–I.

1   steal
2   rob

A   money ☐

B   a bank ☐

C   people ☐

D   passports ☐

E   someone's watch ☐

F   money from people ☐

G   people of their money ☐

H   a security guard ☐

I   money from a security guard ☐

B Now complete these sentences using the words in the box.

rob	steal	robbed	stole	stolen

1 A   Is it possible that someone broke into Tom Hellman's office and tried to ___ something from him?

  B   I don't think so. Nothing was ___ from his office at all.

2 A   No, no. What I mean is perhaps someone killed Hellman because they were trying to ___ him of his money or something.

  B   I've already told you. Nobody ___ anything from his office.

3 A   Are you absolutely sure that he wasn't ___ and then killed?

  B   Yes, I'm sure. Nothing was ___ from him.

4 A   But how can you be sure that he wasn't ___ before he was killed?

  B   He had more than $400 in his pocket. If someone wanted to ___ him, why didn't they ___ that money?

C 👥 With a partner, read aloud the complete conversation in Exercise B. One of you takes role A and the other takes role B.

8 READ & TALK ABOUT IT

A **An American tourist talks about two moments or experiences. One was unpleasant, or bad. The other was pleasant, or good. Connect the two parts of each sentence. Then read the complete sentences aloud.**

1 Six months ago I was travelling `E`

2 I had a lot of money with ☐

3 When we came to my stop, I ☐

4 I put my hand in my pocket, but ☐

5 'Oh, my God,' I thought. 'It's ☐

6 Just then a young woman came running ☐

7 'Excuse me. You dropped this,' she ☐

8 She ran back and got ☐

9 All my money was still ☐

10 I never ☐

A got off the train and started walking up some stairs.

B said and then handed my wallet to me.

C been stolen.'

D my wallet wasn't there.

E on a train in Tokyo.

F in my wallet.

G on the train again.

H up the stairs after me.

I me in my wallet.

J saw the young woman again.

B 🗣 **Now talk about these questions with your partners.**

1 Which moment do you think was very unpleasant for the tourist in Exercise A?

2 Which moment was pleasant?

C 🗣 **Tell your partners about some unpleasant or pleasant moments in your own life. Explain where you were when it happened, and exactly what happened.**

9 🔊 LISTENING

A **Ros Kovalski is being interviewed on a San Francisco radio station. Listen to the interview. Then choose the best way to complete the questions below.**

1 How long ___ a detective?
   A is Ros   B was Ros   C has Ros been

2 What about her father? What ___?
   A did he do   B does he do   C is he doing

3 What ___ to him when Ros was twelve years old?
   A has happened   B happens   C happened

4 What did she ___ her father a year or two before this happened?
   A tell   B say   C explain

5 Why didn't he ___ it was a good idea?
   A thought   B think   C thinking

6 What did she want to ___ out?
   A find   B found   C finding

7 Why does she ___ her job?
   A does   B doing   C do

B 🗣 **Check your answers to Exercise A with your teacher. Then ask your partners the complete questions.**

C 🗣 **Choose at least one question. Talk about it with your partners.**

■ Would you like to do the same job that Ros does? Give reasons for your answer.

■ Describe a job you don't do but which you would like to do.

■ Think about yourself when you were ten or twelve years old. At that time what did you want to be when you grew up?

7 HOW WAS YOUR FLIGHT?

1 👤👤 TALK ABOUT THE PICTURES

1 Tell your partner where you think the people are in each picture.
2 Now describe what the people are doing in each picture.
3 What do you think the people are saying in each picture?

2 CONVERSATION

DAY 3 : WEDNESDAY : MORNING : LONDON AIRPORT

A 🔊 **Listen to the first part of the conversation.**

ROBERT KELLER HAS JUST ARRIVED. SUE O'BRIAN IS THERE TO MEET HIM. SHE WORKS AT THE GCS LONDON OFFICE.

ROBERT   Have you been waiting very long?
SUE   No, I got here about twenty minutes ago. How was your flight?
ROBERT   Everything was all right.
SUE   Did you get any sleep?
ROBERT   A little. Two or three hours.
SUE   Is that all? You must be very tired.
ROBERT   I'll be all right. Now, as you know, I was going to leave on Sunday morning, but now I'm leaving on Saturday morning.
SUE   Yes. That's why the next few days are going to be so busy for you. Everything you were going to do between now and Sunday has been re-arranged so that you can do them before you leave on Saturday.
ROBERT   Good. And what about this evening?
SUE   You're having dinner with Linda Shawcross. Have you met her before?
ROBERT   Yes, I think I met her the last time I was here. She's the head of the Hotline team, isn't she?
SUE   Yes. She wants to discuss several serious problems with you.

B 🔊 **Now listen to the complete conversation, which includes a second part.**

👤👤 **Then discuss these questions with your partners.**

1 Why do you think Sue says 'You *must* be very tired'?
2 Explain why Robert is going to be so busy for the next few days.
3 What do you think Robert and Linda Shawcross are going to talk about this evening?

3 WORDS & MEANINGS

Connect the two parts of each definition (1–5; A–E).

1   If you have *several* problems, you have
2   If you are the *head* of a team, you
3   When you *complain*, you say that you
4   When you say 'I *understand* that several customers have complained about it,' you
5   If you *deal* with customers, you

A   aren't happy about something.
B   mean that other people have told you this.
C   do business with them in some way, and probably have contact with them.
D   four or five perhaps, but not much more than that.
E   are the leader or boss.

4 TALK ABOUT IT

Choose one or two of the questions below and talk about them with your partners.

■   Why do business people often discuss problems with each other in restaurants rather than in the office?

■   At what other places do people sometimes discuss business?

■   Find out from other people where they usually meet friends. At home? Outside the home? If so, where? And why do they meet outside the home?

5 FORM & MEANING

A   **Which pairs of sentences mean more or less the same thing? When there is an important difference, explain the difference.**

▼ GRAMMAR 8A, p. 116; 10A, p. 117
1 A   I'm going to leave the day after tomorrow.
  B   I was going to leave the day after tomorrow.

2 A   I was going to leave tomorrow.
  B   I had planned to leave tomorrow, but I've changed my plans now.

3 A   I'm planning to leave on Friday.
  B   I was planning to leave on Friday.

▼ GRAMMAR 8B, p. 116
4 A   I'm leaving on Friday.
  B   I'm going to leave on Friday.

▼ GRAMMAR 9A, p. 117
5 A   I'll leave tomorrow.
  B   I've just decided to leave tomorrow.

B   **Say the sentences aloud that you think mean the following things.**

A   This is what I've already planned and as far as I know it's still what I will do.
B   This was my plan, but it isn't any more.
C   This is a new decision. It's something that I hadn't planned to do a few moments ago.

C   **Two friends are talking. Say the best way to complete each sentence. Then read the complete conversation aloud with a partner.**

1   Do you have any plans for tomorrow evening? I mean, what ___?
    A do you do   B will you do   C are you doing

2   ___ a friend. Why?
    A I'm going to see   B I'll see   C I see

3   ___ a party. Why don't you come?
    A I'm having   B I'll have   C I have

4   Oh, ___ that. But what about my friend?
    A I'll like   B I like   C I'd like

5   Why ___ you bring your friend, too?
    A don't   B won't   C wouldn't

6   All right, ___ that. Thanks very much.
    A I'm doing   B I'll do   C I do

6 VOCABULARY REVISION

A Study this simple 'picture of time'.

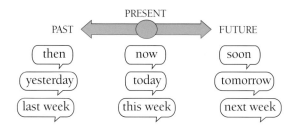

B Now look at the words below. Say 'past', 'present' or 'future' for each one.

1 next month
2 the week after next
3 the day before yesterday
4 this morning
5 three weeks from now
6 three weeks ago
7 in a few years' time
8 soon

C Now complete the sentences using the verbs in brackets (   ). Change the form of the verbs to fit the time. Sometimes more than one form is correct.

EXAMPLE (come) The bus *will come* soon.
The bus *is going to come* soon.
The bus *is coming* soon.

1 *(have)*   We ___ a party next week.
2 *(see)*   When ___ I ___ you again?
3 *(discuss)* We ___ the problem several weeks ago.
4 *(do)*   What ___ you ___ at the moment? I mean, are you busy?
5 *(go)*   I ___ to Japan next month.
6 *(meet)*   I think I ___ Linda Shawcross last month.
7 *(leave)*   I've changed my plans. I ___ on Friday, but now I've decided to stay until Sunday.
8 *(phone)*   I ___ you yesterday evening, but then something happened and I forgot all about it. I'm really sorry.
9 *(leave)*   I wanted to see Linda yesterday evening, but when I got to her office, she ___ already ___.

7 WRITING & PRONUNCIATION

A In each sentence below, one word is written in a special way that gives you a clear idea of the way it is normally spoken. Underline the word that is written in this way. Then say the full form.

EXAMPLE I'm coming.   (I am)

1 I'd like to see you tomorrow.
2 What's Robert doing?
3 What's he done this time?
4 I've never been to London before.
5 What'll we do if it rains tomorrow?
6 I phoned you yesterday but you'd already left.
7 I'd help you if I could.

B 🔊 Look at the eight sentences below. In each of them, there is a *verb form* that in everyday speech is usually pronounced as a weak form. However, that verb is not written as a weak form here. Underline the words, then say the weak form.

EXAMPLE Well, do you like it?   (d'you)

1 Well, what do you think?
2 What does this word mean?
3 I was going to ask you something.
4 Pardon? What did you say?
5 Where are my glasses?
6 What have you done with them?
7 What is happening?
8 What has happened?

C 👤 Now practise saying the eight sentences in Exercise B above.

D 🔊 Say the four words in each group. When does the sound of the underlined letter or letters change?

1 bus   busy   us   discuss
2 is   busy   business   exercise
3 this   is   his   busy
4 arrive   expensive   give   detective
5 arrive   expensive   drive   five
6 drive   expensive   give   detective

8 Read & talk about it

A Read the advertisement for the Cadillac Hotel. (You'll hear more about this hotel later.) Then answer the questions below.

THE CADILLAC HOTEL

Stay where Charlie Chaplin used to stay.

See the Pacific Ocean from your room.
A small, friendly hotel on Venice Beach, Venice, California.
Comfortable rooms, moderate rates.
Close to Los Angeles International Airport.
Lots of good restaurants nearby.
Tours of the Hollywood studios & Disneyland arranged.
Visit the fabulous Getty Art Museum just up the road.
See Beverley Hills and the houses of your favourite stars.

Tel: 310 399 8876
Fax: 310 399 4536

1 Where is the hotel located?
2 Why do people go there?
3 What advantages does the hotel offer?
4 What do you know about the area in which the hotel is located?

B Discuss at least two of these questions with your partners.

1 Talk about some of the different things you would like to do if you stayed at the Cadillac Hotel.

2 How would you get to the hotel from where you are now?

3 What would you take with you? Name at least five different things you would pack in your suitcase.

4 What questions would you ask before reserving a room at this hotel?

5 Why are so many people all over the world interested in the Los Angeles area?

6 Are you personally interested in that area?

7 If your answer to the last question above was 'yes', explain why. If your answer was 'no', explain why not.

9 ◀)) Listening

A A man and a woman are talking on the phone. Listen to their conversation. Then look at the statements below. Which of them are true? Which are false? Correct the false statements so that they are true.

EXAMPLE   The man and the woman both want information about the hotel.
ANSWER   False. She wants information. He is giving the information.

1 She is going to stay at the hotel with a friend.
2 From what she says, it seems that she has stayed at that hotel before.
3 From what the man says, it seems that most of the information in the advertisement is correct.
4 She seems to be interested in art.
5 She is not the person who is going to pay for the room.
6 She is going to send the hotel some important information in a few minutes.
7 Many years ago a very famous film star stayed at the same hotel.

B Connect the two parts of each sentence.

1 The room costs eighty dollars
2 She wants a single room for
3 One of the reasons she wants to stay
4 She can get to the
5 The hotel used to be a house that
6 She is going to fax the number
7 She is also going to fax written

A there is to visit the Getty Art Museum.
B of her credit card and the expiry date.
C plus state tax.
D museum by bus.
E five nights.
F confirmation of the reservation.
G Charlie Chaplin stayed in during the summer.

8 CUSTOMER COMPLAINTS

1 👤👥 TALK ABOUT IT

1 Find out how many people in your class use these things at least once a week.

- a computer ■ a calculator ■ a fax ■ a photocopier
- an automatic ticket machine ■ an electric razor

2 Name at least two other machines you use.
3 Describe in English how to use at least two of these machines.

2 CONVERSATION

A 🔊 Listen to the first part of the conversation.

DAY 3 : WEDNESDAY : EVENING : A LONDON RESTAURANT

ROBERT KELLER IS TALKING TO LINDA SHAWCROSS, THE HEAD OF THE HOTLINE TEAM IN LONDON.

ROBERT   What do the people you deal with say about the test version of RAINBOW 3?

LINDA   Well, what they like about it is that it's very powerful. What they don't like is that it's more difficult to use than RAINBOW 2.

ROBERT   Yes, I know that RAINBOW 2 is slightly more user-friendly.

LINDA   The customers I've spoken to don't say 'slightly more'. They say 'far more'. In fact, they don't find RAINBOW 3 user-friendly at all.

ROBERT   Perhaps if they had more training they wouldn't find it so difficult.

LINDA   That's what I've suggested to them. And I tell them that RAINBOW 3 does far more things than RAINBOW 2 could do. But they all ask the same question.

ROBERT   What question is that?

LINDA   Why can't RAINBOW 3 be powerful and user-friendly at the same time?

B 🔊 Now listen to the complete conversation, which includes a second part.

👤👥 **Then discuss these questions with your partners.**

1 What do Linda's customers say about RAINBOW 3?
2 Why is RAINBOW 3 more difficult to use than RAINBOW 2?
3 What do you think customers really want from RAINBOW 3?
4 Who is Ed Bondy and what does Linda say about him?

3 COMPREHENSION CHECK

A   What are the words in the conversation that mean these things?

1   A product that is perhaps not final or perfect but which customers use so that the makers can find out what those customers think of it.
2   A word you can use about a car with a very big engine or about computer software that does many things.
3   What you do when you give someone an idea to think about.
4   'Easy for the user to use'.

B   Correct the explanations you don't agree with.

1   When people say 'If I *had* more training' or 'If I *had* more time,' they are talking about things they had in the past but no longer have.
2   'Slightly more difficult' means 'a lot more difficult'.
3   If you say someone 'isn't very easy to talk to,' it's usually because you don't think that person really wants to listen.
4   If you say 'I don't think anyone knows him very well,' it means he hasn't got any friends.
5   When someone is your *boss*, you are their manager and they report to you.

4 TALK ABOUT IT

Choose one of the questions below and talk about it with your partners.

■   What methods do makers of the following products use to test their products?
  • cosmetics and perfumes
  • medicines
  • crash helmets
  • car seat belts

■   Think of a questionnaire you have been asked to complete. What were the questions designed to find out?

■   When was the last time you complained about something? What was your complaint? What happened?

5 FORM & MEANING

A   Which pairs of sentences below mean more or less the same thing? When is there an important difference in meaning between the two sentences in a pair?

▼ GRAMMAR 12, p. 118

1 A   All the customers I spoke to say the same thing.
  B   All the customers that I spoke to say the same thing.

2 A   Who are the customers that say this to you?
  B   Who are the customers you say this to?

3 A   Who are the people you deal with?
  B   Who are the people that deal with you?

B   Match the sentences in Exercise A with the meanings below. Remember that in one pair, both sentences mean the same thing.

A   You deal with people. Who are they?
B   People deal with you. Who are they?
C   Customers say this to you. Who are they?
D   You say this to customers. But which customers?
E   I spoke to customers and they all say the same thing.

C   In which of these sentences is it not really necessary to use the word 'that'?

1   Who are the people that you love most?
2   Who are the people that love you most?
3   RAINBOW 3 has some features that make it difficult to use.
4   RAINBOW 3 has some features that RAINBOW 2 didn't have.

D   Complete only the sentences below in which 'that' is really necessary.

1   What are the features ___ make RAINBOW 3 so difficult to use?
2   Tell me about the features ___ RAINBOW 3 has.
3   Who are the people here ___ know you?
4   Who are the people here ___ you know?
5   What is it about this city ___ makes it so popular with tourists?
6   What is it about this city ___ you like so much?
7   Here are three things ___ I did yesterday.
8   Here are three things ___ happened to me.

6 VOCABULARY PRACTICE

A **Look at the picture of Ed Bondy opposite. (You'll learn more about him later.) Sentences 1–8 are things different people say about him. Match those eight sentences with their explanations (A–H).**

1 He's very professional.
2 He's extremely ambitious.
3 He's extremely shy.
4 He can be very moody.
5 He's tight-fisted.
6 He has no sense of humour.
7 He can be very sarcastic.
8 He's a brilliant engineer.

A He never laughs or sees the funny side of life.
B Sometimes he seems very unhappy.
C He has lots of very good technical ideas.
D He doesn't like spending money.
E He knows his job and does it well.
F He wants to be very successful.
G He doesn't find it easy to talk to people he doesn't know or to be with them.
H He sometimes says things like 'That's a wonderful idea' in such a way that you know he doesn't think it is a good idea at all.

B **Here are some things people say about people. Which of them are 'good'? Which are 'bad'? Which are 'not good or bad'?**

- kind ■ generous ■ easy to get along with
- has very low standards ■ lazy ■ talkative
- loves a good joke ■ reliable ■ reserved
- cold as a fish ■ very hard-working
- a slave-driver ■ polite and friendly
- careful with money ■ never says much
- keeps his/her promises ■ honest

C 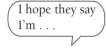 **Look again at all the descriptions in Exercises A and B. Tell your partners the things you hope people say about you and the things you hope they don't say about you.**

> I hope they say I'm . . .

> I hope people never say I'm . . .

7 READ & TALK ABOUT IT

A **Connect the first part of each sentence (1–6) with the second part of that sentence (A–F).**

1 One good thing about Ed Bondy is
2 But one of the bad things about him is that he
3 What some users of this software don't like is that
4 But what other users like is that
5 What most people like about San Francisco is
6 On the other hand, what some people don't like is that the weather

A can be very sarcastic.
B can change very quickly.
C that he's a brilliant engineer.
D that it's a very beautiful and interesting city.
E it can do a lot of things other software programs can't do.
F it isn't very user-friendly.

B **Look at the six complete sentences in Exercise A again. Then see if you can remember how each sentence ends without looking at it. Your partner reads the first part (1–6). You try to remember the second part (A–F).**

C **Work with one or more people. Choose a place, a person or a thing (a book, a machine, a film or something else). Make complete sentences about that place, person or thing. Use sentences like the following:**

One good thing about . . . is that he/she/it is . . .
But one of the bad things about him/her/it is that . . .

What some people like about . . . is that it/she/he . . .
On the other hand, what some people don't like is that it/she/he . . .

8 STRESS & PRONUNCIATION

A Say the five pairs of words with your teacher. Notice that the first word is stressed on the first syllable and the second word is stressed on the second syllable.

1 <u>ver</u>sion   com<u>plain</u>
2 <u>fea</u>ture   sug<u>gest</u>
3 <u>care</u>ful   re<u>tired</u>
4 <u>prom</u>ise   suc<u>cess</u>
5 <u>mon</u>ey   po<u>lite</u>

B 👤👤 🔊 Now work with a partner. Say the three words in each group (1–8). One of the three words is stressed on a different syllable. Which word is the 'different' word? In the different word is the stress on the first or the second syllable?

EXAMPLE   version   complain   feature
ANSWER   com<u>plain</u> (second syllable)

1 retire   polite   careful
2 moody   success   suggest
3 engine   reason   expect
4 honest   humour   again
5 depressed   funny   worried
6 below   above   standard
7 software   hardware   advice
8 practice   arrange   confirm

C Now ask your teacher to say the words above. Does your teacher agree with you about the 'different' word and which syllable is stressed in that word?

D 🔊 Now say these four groups of three words. This time it is not the stress that is different but the sound of the underlined letters. In which word is the sound of the underlined letters different?

1 pr<u>o</u>mise   pr<u>o</u>gram   j<u>o</u>ke
2 m<u>oo</u>dy   f<u>oo</u>d   f<u>oo</u>t
3 g<u>oo</u>d   f<u>oo</u>d   p<u>u</u>t
4 kn<u>ow</u>   kn<u>ow</u>ledge   pr<u>o</u>gram

9 🔊 LISTENING

A Robert Keller and Linda Shawcross are still talking. Listen to their conversation. Then choose the best way to complete the questions.

1 How well ___ Linda know Ed Bondy?
   A is   B has   C does

2 Who is the other person ___?
   A they're talking about   B that they are talking
   C about that they are talking

3 When did Silvina Arcante ___ back to Argentina?
   A gone   B go   C went

4 Why ___ she quit her job at GCS?
   A was   B is   C did

5 Does Robert ___ her?
   A remember   B remembered   C remembering

6 Did he ___ her?
   A liked   B likes   C like

7 Are Silvina and Linda ___?
   A good friend   B good friends   C of a good friend

8 What ___ at the moment?
   A is Silvina doing   B does Silvina do   C does Silvina

9 Why do you think ___ wants her telephone number?
   A does Robert   B Robert   C Robert does

10 Does Robert hope to see Silvina when he ___ back to San Francisco?
   A go   B will go   C has gone

B Here are answers to six of the questions. Which six?

A Last year.
B Yes, he did. Very much.
C She's attending a conference in San Francisco.
D Yes, of course he remembers her.
E I don't know. Robert and Linda don't give a reason.
F Yes. he does. He's going to ask her secretary where she's staying.

C 👤 Ask your partner the complete questions in Exercise A.

9 AN UNEXPECTED VISITOR

1 👥 TALK ABOUT IT

1 Who are the two people?
2 What do you know about them?
3 Where are they?
4 What do you think they are going to talk about?

2 ▥))) READING

DAY 4 : THURSDAY : AFTERNOON : ED BONDY'S OFFICE : GCS

The phone on Ed Bondy's desk rang. He answered it.

'I'm sorry to disturb you, Mr Bondy, but there's someone here to see you,' his secretary told him

'What do you mean? I'm not expecting anyone.'

At that moment a young woman in a dark jacket walked into his office.

'Who are you? What are you doing in my office?' Bondy demanded.

'My name's Kovalski. Do you mind if I ask you a few questions?' the young woman said quietly, and showed him a police badge.

'I'm very busy!'

'I'm very busy, too, Mr Bondy.'

Kovalski took a long look at Bondy's face. His mouth was small.

'How did you get in here?' he asked angrily.

'Through the door, of course.'

Bondy's mouth became even smaller.

She sat down in front of his desk.

'Why did Tom Hellman phone you late last Sunday?'

Bondy looked surprised.

'How did you know that?'

'The telephone company has records. I looked at them. Now, could you tell me why he phoned you?'

Bondy seemed to be thinking.

'He wanted my advice about a personal problem.'

'Would you mind telling me what kind of a personal problem?'

Bondy did not answer immediately.

'His wife had left him,' he finally said.

Kovalski stood up and walked towards the door. Just before she opened it, she turned around.

'One more question.'

'What?'

'Was Tom Hellman a personal friend of yours?'

'I was his boss, not his friend.'

Sergeant Kovalski looked directly into Bondy's eyes.

'Thank you for your time,' she said and left as suddenly as she had come.

Look again at the questions in Exercise 1. Now that you have read the text, do you want to change any of your answers?

3 COMPREHENSION CHECK

A Find the words in the text in Exercise 2 that mean these things.

1 To stop someone working or sleeping.
2 To ask in a way that shows clearly you expect an answer.
3 Another way of asking 'Is it all right if I . . . ?'
4 The way you feel when something happens that you didn't expect.

B 👤👤 What do you think is the missing word in each question below? If you aren't sure, ask your teacher.

1 Do you think that Bondy and Kovalski ___ ever met each other before she walked into his office?
2 Do you think she ___ made an appointment with him before she came?
3 Do you think that people often walk into Bondy's office without ___ an appointment with him first?
4 Why do you think Kovalski didn't ___ an appointment with him first?
5 Do you think Bondy ___ telling the truth when he said that Hellman wanted his advice about a 'personal problem'?

C 👤👤 Now take turns with your partners in asking or answering the five questions in Exercise B. Here are three possible answers, but only one is a possible answer to all the questions.

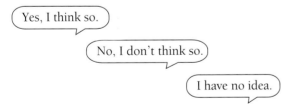

Yes, I think so.

No, I don't think so.

I have no idea.

4 👤👤 TALK ABOUT IT

■ Why do you think Kovalski wanted to look at Bondy and not just talk to him on the phone?

■ Who are the people you often see without making an appointment first?

■ Who are the people you usually make an appointment with before you see them?

5 FORM & MEANING

A 👤👤 What's the difference?

▼ GRAMMAR 5 & 6, p. 115

1 A 'What are you doing in my office?' he asked.
  B 'What are you doing in my office?' he demanded.

2 A I'm going to ask you a few questions.
  B Do you mind if I ask you a few questions?

3 A Could you tell me why Hellman phoned you so late?
  B Tell me why Hellman phoned you so late.

4 A Why did he want to talk to you?
  B Would you mind telling me why he wanted to talk to you?

Look at pairs 2, 3 and 4 again. Then repeat the sentences in the three pairs that can sound like *demands* and not *polite requests*.

Now repeat the sentences in pairs 2, 3 and 4 that sound more like polite requests.

B Say the best way of completing each request for information.

1 Do you mind ___ you some questions?
  A that I ask B if I ask C me to ask

2 Do you remember the last time ___ to Hellman?
  A you spoke B did you speak C you speak

3 Can you tell me what ___ about?
  A did you speak B you speak C you spoke

4 Would you mind ___ me why he wanted your advice?
  A to tell B that you tell C telling

5 I'd like ___ answer just a few more questions.
  A you to B that you C you will

6 Could you tell me how well ___ Tom Hellman's wife?
  A knew you B did you know C you knew

7 Do you have any idea why ___ him?
  A she left B has she left C did she leave

8 Can you tell me how ___ contact her?
  A can I B I can C do I

6 CONVERSATION SKILLS

A Connect the two parts of each question.

1 Do you mind if I
2 How often do you go
3 When do you
4 How do you usually pay for
5 Where do
6 Do you ever pay
7 Do you remember the last time
8 What did you

A you buy food?
B you paid for something by cheque?
C by cheque?
D ask you a few questions?
E what you buy?
F shopping?
G pay for by cheque?
H do your shopping?

B Now connect the eight questions in Exercise A with these answers. There are two answers here for one of the questions above.

1 Yes, I do. Sometimes but not very often.
2 Cash. Credit card. It depends on what I buy.
3 A computer. It was very expensive.
4 No, I don't. Go ahead.
5 Usually at the weekend, or Thursday evenings, after work.
6 Twice a week, or sometimes more often.
7 At the local supermarket.
8 By cheque.
9 Yes. About a week ago.

C ＊＊ Now take turns practising the questions and answers above with your partners.

D ＊＊ Now ask your partners the same questions again. But this time your partners give their own answers, and not the answers in Exercise B.

Do you mind if I ask you a few questions?

I'm sorry. I'm very busy at the moment.

7 VOCABULARY PRACTICE

A Say aloud the four words in each group. Then say which word you think doesn't belong with the other three. Sometimes it is possible to say that two words do not belong with the other two. But it is always possible to connect *one* of those two words with the other two words in the same group.

1 jacket books sweater jeans
2 books clothes read write
3 clothes shoes carry wear
4 books bags carry wear
5 questions ask answer watch
6 telephone ask answer use
7 make appointments mistakes suicide
8 jobs exercises do make

B ＊＊ Now explain why one of the words does not belong with the other three.

EXAMPLE   jacket books sweater jeans
ANSWER

'Books' doesn't belong because you can't wear them.

8 ◆)) PRONUNCIATION

A When does the sound of the underlined letter or letters change?

1 cl<u>o</u>thes th<u>o</u>se <u>o</u>ther <u>o</u>wn
2 m<u>o</u>ney <u>o</u>ther b<u>u</u>s sh<u>o</u>p
3 cl<u>o</u>thes m<u>o</u>dern sh<u>o</u>p j<u>o</u>b
4 <u>ch</u>eque ques<u>ti</u>on <u>ti</u>me <u>ch</u>ange
5 <u>sh</u>oes <u>ch</u>oose <u>ch</u>ampagne ma<u>ch</u>ine
6 shoe<u>s</u> book<u>s</u> bu<u>s</u> me<u>ss</u>age
7 <u>sh</u>oes <u>th</u>ose <u>ch</u>oose hou<u>s</u>e
8 ri<u>c</u>e ri<u>s</u>e ni<u>c</u>e like<u>s</u>

B Now say all the words in Exercise A that have these sounds.

1 the 'o' sound in <u>o</u>wn
2 the 'u' sound in b<u>u</u>s
3 the 'o' sound in j<u>o</u>b
4 the 'ch' sound in <u>ch</u>eque
5 the 'sh' sound in <u>sh</u>oe
6 the 'z' sound in shoe<u>s</u>
7 the 's' sound in hou<u>s</u>e

9 GRAMMAR REVISION

A In which pairs of questions is there an important difference in meaning? When is the meaning more or less the same?

▼ GRAMMAR 2A–D, p. 113

1 A What was Bondy doing when Kovalski walked into his office?

  B What did Bondy do when Kovalski walked into his office?

2 A Did she make an appointment when she walked into his office?

  B Had she made an appointment when she walked into his office?

3 A Why did she want to see him?

  B What did she want to talk to him about?

4 A Why did she want to see him?

  B Why did she want to look at him?

B Which sentence above has the following meaning?

A What happened immediately after Kovalski walked into Bondy's office?

B Did Kovalski make an appointment before she went to his office?

C What was it about his face or appearance that interested her?

C Use the words in brackets ( ) to complete each sentence. Change the form of the word to fit the sentence.

1 Before Kovalski (*walk*) ___ into Bondy's office, she (*never seen*) ___ him before.

2 Bondy was surprised when Kovalski walked into his office because she (*not make*) ___ an appointment.

3 When she (*come*) ___ in, Bondy (*sit*) ___ at his desk.

4 'What are you doing in my office?' he (*demand*) ___ when she (*come*) ___ in.

10))) LISTENING

A You are going to hear two separate telephone conversations. Before you listen to the first conversation, study these questions.

1 Who do you think the woman is?

2 What time of day do you think it is?

3 Why is the man phoning?

4 What do you think he is going to do after he finishes the call?

5 Do you think this conversation takes place before or after Sergeant Kovalski walks into Ed Bondy's office? Give reasons for your answer.

🖤 **Now listen to the first conversation and then discuss the questions above with your partners.**

B Before you listen to the second conversation, study these questions.

1 One of the women in the conversation is the same as the woman in the first conversation. Who do you think the second caller is?

2 What exactly do you think the caller wants to find out?

3 Why do you think the caller doesn't want to make an appointment to see Bondy?

4 What do you think is the connection between the second call and the text on page 40?

🖤 **Now listen to the second conversation and then discuss the questions above with your partners.**

C Complete the conversation below. Then practise it with a partner.

A I'd **1** ___ to see Mr Bondy this afternoon.

B I'm **2** ___ that he's very **3** ___ then. But perhaps I can fit you **4** ___ tomorrow morning.

A No, the only **5** ___ I'm free is this afternoon.

B I'm terribly sorry, but that isn't **6** ___.

A Oh, well, perhaps I can **7** ___ one of my meetings tomorrow morning. When can Mr Bondy **8** ___ me tomorrow?

B Can you be here **9** ___ nine-thirty?

A Yes, I **10** ___. Thanks.

10 SECURITY ARRANGEMENTS

1 👤👤 TALK ABOUT THE PICTURES

1 What do you see in picture 1?
2 Why do companies have such things?
3 What do you think Sergeant Kovalski is talking to the man about in picture 2?
4 Where do you think Sergeant Kovalski is in picture 3?
5 Why is she there?

2 CONVERSATION

A 🔊 **Listen to the first part of the conversation.**

DAY 4 : THURSDAY : AFTERNOON : GCS : SECURITY

KOVALSKI Good afternoon, Mr Tucker.

TUCKER Afternoon, Sergeant. What can I do for you today?

KOVALSKI Sorry to bother you again, but I'd like to ask you a few more questions about security arrangements.

TUCKER Go ahead, Sergeant.

KOVALSKI How do you keep a check on visitors?

TUCKER That's what the security cameras are for. There's at least one camera in every corridor, so that we can see who's in the building and where they go.

KOVALSKI And you keep records of who comes and goes, don't you?

TUCKER Of course we do, Sergeant. Written and visual records, too.

KOVALSKI Visual records? On videotape?

TUCKER Yep.

KOVALSKI Would you mind telling me a little more about the written records?

TUCKER All visitors have to sign in. They're given a visitor's badge. When they leave, they leave the badge at reception. We record the exact time they arrive and leave so that later – if we need to – we can see how long they were in the building.

KOVALSKI Thanks. You've been very helpful . . . Oh, just one last thing, Mr Tucker . . .

B 🔊 **Now listen to the complete conversation, which includes a second part.**

👤👤 **Then discuss these questions with your partners.**

1 Do you think Kovalski and Tucker have talked to each other before? Read aloud something from the conversation that helps you answer this question.
2 What exactly do you think Mr Tucker's job is?
3 Was anything different about Hellman's office on the day he died? If so, what? And why?

3 COMPREHENSION CHECK

Do you agree with all these explanations? Correct the explanations you don't agree with.

1 If you can go in and out of a building and nobody stops you or asks you what you want, the *security arrangements* are very good.
2 If you *keep a check* on someone, you watch what they do.
3 You *sign in* when you write your name in a visitor's book or other document.
4 A *record* of something can only be written, not spoken or in any other form.
5 *Visual records* make it possible to see something before it happens.
6 A *corridor* is the passage between different offices.
7 If I say 'Hellman *was supposed* to move from his office at the end of this week,' I mean that was the plan but it didn't happen that way.

4 TALK ABOUT IT

Choose one or more of the following and discuss possible answers with your partners.

■ Describe what you imagine to be a typical working day for Mr Tucker.

■ Imagine that you are going to see someone who has an office in the building Mr Tucker works in. Describe some of the things you do when you go in and when you leave.

■ Describe the security arrangements in a place where you work, have worked or have visited.

■ What kind of visual records do you have of your past life? Describe some of them. If you look at them, what exactly do you see?

5 FORM & MEANING

A **In the sentences below, two ideas are connected. One idea is *what* we do or want to do. The other idea is *why* we do it. Underline the word or words that connect these two ideas. In sentence 1, this has already been done for you.**

▼ GRAMMAR 14 & 15, pp. 119–120

1 We have security cameras in every corridor <u>because</u> we want to keep a check on visitors.

2 We want to keep a check on visitors. That's why we have security cameras in every corridor.

3 We have security cameras in every corridor in order to keep a check on visitors.

4 We have security cameras in every corridor so that we can keep a check on visitors.

B **What do you think are the missing words below? Connect the two parts of a sentence or the two sentences in a pair. Remember that sometimes only one word is missing, but sometimes more than one word is missing.**

1 Sergeant Kovalski went to see Mr Tucker ___ she wanted to ask him a few questions.
2 She went to see him ___ she could ask him a few questions.
3 She went to see him ___ to ask him a few questions.
4 She wanted to ask him a few questions. ___ she went to see him.

C **Connect the pair of sentences or parts of sentences.**

1 I went to see Ed Bondy the other day in order to
2 I wanted to talk to him because
3 I had to sign in first, of course.
4 They gave me a badge
5 There are cameras in every corridor so that

A That's why I went to reception.
B they can see where visitors go.
C so that people would know I was a visitor.
D get some technical information.
E he's the Technical Director.

6 VOCABULARY PRACTICE

A Look at sentences 1–6. Then match them with sentences A–F. Sometimes two sentences in 1–6 mean more or less the same thing.

1 Keep this.
2 Keep a record of your expenses.
3 Please record this conversation.
4 Copy it.
5 Sign it.
6 Save it.

A Write your name on it.
B Write down all the money you spend.
C Don't throw it away or lose it.
D Don't spend or waste it.
E Write, draw or do something so that it looks just like something else.
F Put it on tape or film.

B 👥 Practise saying these sentences aloud with a partner. Notice which part of the words *record* and *records* is stressed each time.

1 Do you keep <u>record</u>s?
2 Are you going to re<u>cord</u> this?
3 Did you re<u>cord</u> it?
4 Let me look at the <u>record</u>.
5 There's something wrong with these <u>record</u>s.
6 Mr Tucker always re<u>cord</u>s the time each visitor arrives and leaves.

C 👥 Which word is better? Say it.

1 Where do you ___ your records?
   ■ save ■ keep

2 How much money do you ___ every month?
   ■ save ■ keep

3 Please ___ your name here.
   ■ copy ■ sign

4 Could you make a ___ of this document for me?
   ■ copy ■ record

5 I can ___ your voice on tape.
   ■ copy ■ record

6 It's important to ___ accurate records of how much you earn and spend.
   ■ copy ■ keep

7 READING

A Silvina Arcante will be a very important person in our story. She is from Buenos Aires, in Argentina, and she is an independent consultant.

'I advise companies on the best use of their computer hardware and software. I used to work for a large international company. The job itself was very interesting and well-paid, too. However, about eighteen months ago, I decided to quit.

'One of the things I like best about the way I live now is that I make all the most important decisions in my own life. I'm not saying that I can do anything I want. Nobody can. And like everybody else, sometimes I have to do things I don't want to do. Being your own boss isn't easy. But it's a lot better than working for someone else. That's the way I feel, at least.

'There is one thing about being an independent consultant that I don't like. I have to travel a lot. I don't like travelling, especially by car, and I don't like flying very much, either. I used to walk to work. When I worked for that large company, I mean. That was one of the best things about that job. I love walking. It's very good exercise. I haven't been getting enough exercise lately. I'm too busy.'

B Which statements below are true and which are false? Read something from the text in Exercise A that you think gives you the answer.

1 Silvina works for a large international company.
2 She doesn't say why she left her last job.
3 She feels that in at least one important way she is 'freer' now than she used to be.
4 She usually walks to work.
5 She is not very happy when she is on a plane.
6 She would like to get more exercise.

8 QUICK REVISION

A Which sentences below tell you only about something that happened in the past and have no clear connection with the present?

1 She advises companies on the best use of their computer hardware and software.
2 She has been an independent consultant for more than a year.
3 She worked for a large company for more than five years.
4 She used to walk to work every day.
5 She usually starts work very early.
6 She hasn't been getting very much exercise lately.

B 👤 Think of ways to complete these questions about Silvina.

1 What ___ she think is better about the way she lives now?
2 Why ___ she decide to quit her last job?
3 ___ she do anything she wants?
4 Does she ___ travelling by car?
5 Does she walk ___ much ___ she used to?
6 Why ___ she been ___ very much exercise lately?

C 👥 Now ask your partners the complete questions in Exercise B. The answer to one question is 'I don't know'.

9 👥 TALK ABOUT IT

■ Tell your partners about something you don't do as often as you used to. Then explain why you don't do it as often as you used to.

■ Think of something you would like to do more often than you do now. Tell your partners what it is and why you would like to do it more often.

■ How many differences can you find between yourself and Silvina? Tell your partner about them.

> Silvina has to travel a lot, but I don't have to travel at all.

10 🔊 LISTENING

A Robert Keller is very tired at the end of a busy day. However, he has a very important message for someone. Listen. Then answer the questions below.

1 Where is Robert?
2 Where is the person he is phoning?
3 Who is the person Robert has a message for?
4 Where is that person?
5 In your own words, repeat the most important information in the message.

B 👥 The message below is the fax (translated from Spanish) that was sent just after the conversation. Do you and your partners think it is correct in all its details? Listen to the conversation again if necessary. Then make any changes you think are necessary.

From:	Paula Santander
	Buenos Aires, Argentina
To:	Silvina Arcante
	Pacific Orient Hotel, San Francisco
Pages:	1 including this cover

Mr Robert Keller phoned from London today. He has a very important message for you and wants to meet you Saturday afternoon in the coffee-shop at the Button Hotel in London at three p.m. The telephone number is 0171 462 900635. I told Mr Keller that London is very far from San Francisco. He said he knows but I had the impression he thinks you will fly there to see him.

11 TALK ABOUT IT

👥 Choose a question. Discuss it with a partner.

■ How much time do you spend talking to people on the phone every day?

■ What are the advantages of fax messages compared with telephone calls?

■ Find out if anybody uses the Internet or e-mail. What kind of information do they get?

11 JUST AFTER MIDNIGHT

1 👥 TALK ABOUT THE PICTURES

1 Who is the man in the telephone booth?
2 Describe to your partners what you think the woman is like.
3 What do you think they are talking about?

2))) READING

DAY 4/5 : THURSDAY/FRIDAY : SAN FRANCISCO

Ed Bondy glanced at his watch. It was just after midnight and he was standing in a public phone booth in front of a gas station. The phone at the other end began to ring. Bondy kept looking around as he waited. Finally, a woman answered. She didn't sound happy.

'Hello?'

'It's me. I need to talk to you,' Bondy said.

'Jesus! Do you know what time it is?'

'It's important. I wouldn't be phoning now if it weren't. A detective came to see me today.'

'Why? What did he want?' the woman asked. She had an English accent.

'It was a *she*, not a *he*. She asked me about Hellman. She wanted to know how well I knew him. She asked me why he phoned me so late last Sunday night.'

'She knew? How did she know about that?'

'From the records of the telephone company, I suppose. You and I have to meet. We have to talk about this.'

The woman didn't say anything.

'Are you listening?' Bondy shouted.

'Calm down, Ed. Control yourself.'

Bondy took a deep breath. He looked around again. A car drove past in the rain.

'All right. Let's meet. The question is where. It would be very bad if someone saw us together in San Francisco or here in Portland,' the woman told him.

3 COMPREHENSION CHECK

A Find the words in the text that mean these things.

1   To look at something quickly, for a moment or so.
2   Pick up the telephone when it rings and speak.
3   The impression you have from someone's voice about the way they feel.
4   Information in a written form that you can look at later so that you can see who phoned, who said what, how much money was spent, etc.
5   To speak in a very loud voice.
6   Two ways of saying 'You're angry or excited. Don't be like that.'
7   The air you take into your lungs.

B 👥 Work with a partner. Choose at least two of the questions below and answer them.

1   Why do you think Ed went to a public telephone in order to make the call? Why didn't he use his phone at home?
2   Who do you think the woman could be?
3   Why do you think Ed phoned her so late?
4   Why does she think it would be bad if someone saw them together? Can you think of at least two possible explanations?

C 👥 Change partners. Find out what questions in Exercise B your new partner answered. Did your new partner answer any of the same questions that you answered? If so, is there any difference in his or her answer? On the other hand, perhaps your partner answered completely different questions. If so, do you agree with those answers?

4 FORM & MEANING

A 👥 The three sentences below look similar. However, each sentence has a different meaning. Can you explain that difference?

▼ GRAMMAR 16A, p. 120
1   I wouldn't be phoning if it weren't important.
2   I don't phone if it isn't important.

▼ GRAMMAR 17A–B, p. 121
3   I won't phone if it isn't important.

B 👥 Here are three slightly different ways of saying each of the three things above. Which sentence above, 1, 2 or 3 means the following?

A   I never phone people if there is no really important reason for phoning them.
B   I will phone you only if there is an important reason for phoning you.
C   I have an important reason for phoning now. That is why I'm phoning.

C Here are some more examples of similar sentences. Say the words that you think best complete each sentence.

1   I think the reason Ed is phoning is because he is very worried about something. He wouldn't be phoning if he ___ very worried.
    A isn't   B weren't   C would be

2   I'm sure he knows the woman well. He wouldn't phone her so late if he ___ know her well.
    A doesn't   B didn't   C hasn't

3   I don't understand why he is using a public telephone. If I ___ him, I'd use my own phone at home.
    A were   B am   C would be

4   Bondy's very angry. He ___ shout if he felt calm.
    A didn't   B wouldn't   C doesn't

5   And he wouldn't keep looking around if he ___ nervous.
    A isn't   B wouldn't be   C weren't

6   In my country, people phone other people only if they ___ an important reason.
    A will have   B have   C would have

5 VOCABULARY PRACTICE

A 👥 **Match the first part of each sentence (1–7) with the best way to complete that sentence (A–G).**

1 When you *look around*, you
2 When you *glance at* something, you
3 When you *look for* something, you
4 You *stare at* something only if you
5 If you *look* something *up*, you
6 If you *examine* it, you
7 If you *check* something, you

A are probably using a dictionary or a phone book.
B look at it very quickly.
C see if there are any mistakes or if there is anything wrong with it.
D don't know where it is and want to find it.
E look at it very carefully, and perhaps use special instruments to do it.
F look in front, to the left and right and perhaps behind you.
G are very interested in it or if you think there is something strange or unusual about it.

B **Now use words/phrases from Exercise A to complete the sentences below. Sometimes only one word is necessary, and sometimes you need two.**

1 Excuse me. I'm ___ Post Street. Do you know where it is?
2 Before you pay a bill, you should ___ it and make sure there are no mistakes in it.
3 When you arrive in the United States from a foreign country, someone usually ___ your passport and perhaps your luggage, too.
4 Before you cross the street, ___ and make sure no cars are coming towards you very fast.
5 Why is that man over there ___ you? Do you know him? Does he know you?
6 Can I borrow your dictionary? I want to ___ some words I don't know.

6 PRONUNCIATION & INTONATION

A **Say these words separately.**

at   was   of   the   to   and

B 🔊 **Now listen to the sentences below. The underlined words are given the most stress. What about the words from Exercise A? How does the sound change when these words are not stressed?**

1 Ed glanced at his watch.
2 It was just after midnight.
3 He was in a phone booth in front of a gas station.
4 The phone at the other end.
5 The phone at the other end began to ring.
6 The phone at the other end began to ring and ring.

C **Now look at the sentences below, which Ed Bondy or the woman said. Underline one or two words you think are stressed in each sentence. Then say the whole sentence aloud, in more or less the same way you think Bondy or the woman said it.**

1 A detective came to see me today.
2 What did he want?
3 It was a she, not a he.
4 She asked me about Hellman.
5 She asked me why he phoned me.
6 How did she know about that?
7 We have to talk about this.

D 🔊 **Listen to the sentences in Exercise C. Then read the sentences aloud again.**

7 ◀)) LISTENING

A **Listen to the conversation between Ed Bondy and the woman. Her name is Andrea. Write B (for Bondy) or A (for Andrea) in the box after each question below.**

1   Who says it would be very bad if someone saw them together in San Francisco or Portland?   `A`
2   Who suggests a place in another city to meet?   ☐
3   Who thinks this city is in a country far away?   ☐
4   Who will perhaps have a problem if they meet on Sunday?   ☐
5   Who has to find an excuse to get away from an important meeting if it lasts too long?   ☐
6   Who is going to be on a plane for about an hour on Saturday evening?   ☐
7   Who is going to reserve a hotel room?   ☐

B **Connect the two parts of each question.**

1   Why doesn't Andrea want
2   Where are Andrea and Bondy
3   Why doesn't Bondy want to
4   How is he

A   going to get there?
B   to meet in San Francisco or Portland?
C   meet there?
D   going to meet?

C 👥 **Now ask your partners the complete questions in Exercise B.**

8 QUICK REVISION

In each sentence below, there is one word that should not be in the sentence. Underline that word.

1   Where will we meet us again?
2   How long will it take to Ed to get to Los Angeles?
3   I'll be at the hotel when you will get there.
4   I'm going to tell to you this once more.
5   Shut yourself up and listen!
6   Where do people in your country usually meet to discuss about business?

9 TALK ABOUT IT

👥 **Discuss which of the four places you think is the best place to meet for the four groups of people. Give reasons for choosing or not choosing each place. (See USEFUL LANGUAGE below.)**

THE PLACES

1   THE CADILLAC HOTEL
     A small, comfortable and not very expensive hotel near good restaurants with a beautiful view of the Pacific Ocean. There is an airport not far away.

2   'AWAY FROM IT ALL'
     An old hotel in the mountains, far away from any city or town, with only one narrow road leading to it. Nobody has lived in it for the last six months.

3   METRO-INTERNET
     A modern coffee-shop close to the centre of the city. Good coffee, light lunches and snacks. No background music. Tables can be reserved for an hour.

4   'DOWNTOWN'
     A large restaurant that serves good food at low prices near the main train station in a large city in the centre of the country.

THE PEOPLE

■   Two business people who work in offices at different ends of a city want to meet for about half an hour and discuss something.

■   Four bank robbers who are planning their next robbery. There are pictures of the robbers in public places everywhere.

■   Ten men and women who live in different parts of the country. They went to the same university five years ago. This is their first meeting in five years.

■   A young couple want to spend their first holiday together. They don't have a car.

USEFUL LANGUAGE

> I think the best place for . . . to meet is . . . because . . .

> I don't think . . . is a good place for . . . to meet because it . . .

> In my opinion, . . . is/isn't a good place for . . . to meet because . . .

12 I DON'T BELIEVE HIM

1 👥 TALK ABOUT IT

1　Find out what your partners remember about the two people in the picture.
2　What happened when one of the people went to see Ed Bondy? Tell your partners about that meeting. Where did they meet? What was said?

2 CONVERSATION

A 🔊 Listen to the first part of the conversation.

DAY 5 : FRIDAY : AROUND MIDNIGHT : SFPD

KOVALSKI　Bondy says Hellman had a personal problem. He says that's why Hellman phoned him around midnight on Sunday.

FERRANTE　You mean, Hellman wanted to talk about the problem with Bondy?

KOVALSKI　That's what Bondy says. But I don't believe him.

FERRANTE　Before you tell me why, let me get some more coffee.

KOVALSKI　I don't know how you can drink that stuff.

FERRANTE　Well, at least it's hot. Are you sure you don't want some?

KOVALSKI　No, thanks.

FERRANTE　So, why don't you believe Bondy?

KOVALSKI　Bondy was Hellman's boss, not his friend. If Hellman wanted to discuss a problem with him, it must have been a problem with his work.

FERRANTE　What could that problem have been?

KOVALSKI　I don't know. But it must have been very serious.

FERRANTE　But what does this have to do with the case? You don't think Bondy killed Hellman, do you?

KOVALSKI　No. He couldn't have killed him. He was checking in at the airport when Hellman died. He had to go to a conference in Portland.

FERRANTE　Well, why are you so interested in this late phone call, then?

KOVALSKI　Bondy lied to me. I want to know why.

B 🔊 Now listen to the complete conversation, which includes a second part.

👥 **Then discuss these questions with your partners.**

1　What doesn't Kovalski believe?
2　Why doesn't she believe it?
3　Why doesn't she think Bondy killed Hellman?
4　Why does Ferrante say near the end of the conversation 'There's an awful lot you don't know'?

3 COMPREHENSION CHECK

A Find the words in the conversation that mean these things.

1 Twelve o'clock when it is dark.
2 Anything that you can see or touch.
3 What you do just after you arrive at a hotel or an airport.
4 A meeting at which at least two – and often far more – people exchange ideas, etc.
5 Not tell the truth.

B Complete the following questions that Ferrante asks Kovalski in the second part of the conversation (that is not on the page).

1 ___ they have any security arrangements there?
2 How did the murderer ___ into the building?
3 How ___ it possible for the murderer to ___ up to Hellman's office?
4 How ___ he get ___ of the building?
5 Why ___ anybody ___ him?

C Ask your partner the complete questions in Exercise B. Can your partner remember Kovalski's answers and how she changed her answer to the fifth question?

4 TALK ABOUT IT

Choose at least one question below and talk about it with your partner.

- The President of the United States is going to visit the place where you have your English lessons. What kind of security arrangements do you think there will be on the day of the visit? Describe them.

- Have you ever been stopped on your way into or out of a building? If so, who stopped you? What did you do and say?

- How could Hellman's murderer have got into and out of the building without being stopped?

- What is Kovalski going to do to find the answers to the last question above?

5 FORM & MEANING

A Which pairs of sentences mean more or less the same thing? When is there an important difference in meaning?

▼ GRAMMAR 19C & 20A, p. 122

1 A I don't believe that Bondy killed Hellman.
  B Bondy couldn't kill Hellman.

2 A I tried to contact you yesterday, but it wasn't possible.
  B I couldn't contact you yesterday.

3 A The students tried to do the exercise, but it was too difficult.
  B They couldn't have done the exercise.

4 A I don't believe you did it.
  B You couldn't have done it.

▼ GRAMMAR 20C, p. 122

5 A I'm sure it was very difficult for you.
  B It must have been very difficult for you.

6 A I'm sure you love your mother very much.
  B You must have loved your mother very much.

B Read aloud the sentences above that mean the following things.

1 I don't believe that the students did the exercise. It isn't possible that they did it.
2 I have a very strong feeling that when your mother was alive, you loved her very much.
3 Bondy tried to kill Hellman, but for some reason it wasn't possible for him to do it.

C Say the correct words to complete each sentence.

1 I don't believe Bondy killed Hellman. He was in another city. He couldn't ___ him.
  A kill   B has killed   C have killed

2 I'm sure that Bondy didn't kill Hellman. He couldn't _____ it. It was someone else.
  A has done   B have done   C done

3 If Hellman killed himself because he had a problem, it must _____ a very serious problem.
  A have been   B has been   C be

4 Bondy tried to kill Hellman but someone stopped him before he could _____ it.
  A has done   B have done   C do

53

6 VOCABULARY PRACTICE

A 👥 **The verb 'get' has at least twenty different meanings. Here are only six of them (A–F). With a partner, match each meaning with one of the complete sentences (1–6).**

A   arrive in a place
B   go from one place to another place
C   buy
D   become; that is, to change in some way from one state or condition to another
E   receive
F   take, go by, catch

1   What's the best way to get from here to the airport?
2   Get the train. It's faster than the bus.
3   Did you get my message?
4   If you take a plane at midnight, you can get to New York by nine tomorrow morning.
5   Keep calm. Don't get angry.
6   Where can I get some stamps?

B   Now connect the two parts of each question.

1   How do you
2   Where can I get a sandwich or
3   What's the fastest way
4   When was the last time
5   Do you often get letters or
6   What would you do if you had to

A   something to eat?
B   get to New York by nine tomorrow evening?
C   postcards from your friends?
D   to get from here to New York?
E   usually get here?
F   you got really angry?

C   Here are possible answers to three of the questions above. Which three?

1   By plane, of course.
2   By train.
3   Yes, sometimes. Do you?

D 👥 **Ask your partners the complete questions in Exercise B.**

7 👥 READ & TALK ABOUT IT

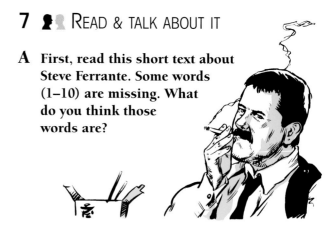

A   First, read this short text about Steve Ferrante. Some words (1–10) are missing. What do you think those words are?

Steve Ferrante lives in a small house near Golden Gate Bridge. San Francisco isn't a large city, so it usually doesn't **1** ___ him more than twenty minutes to **2** ___ to work in downtown San Francisco. Steve works irregular hours. He usually **3** ___ to work at eight in the morning and sometimes leaves at six or seven in the evening. Sometimes he works even later and doesn't **4** ___ home until after midnight.

Steve drinks a lot of coffee – about nine cups a day. He **5** ___ it from a machine in his office. He used to be a heavy smoker, thirty or more cigarettes a day. But now he's trying to cut **6** ___ on his smoking. His wife keeps telling him he should give it **7** ___ completely, but he can't. Steve usually has lunch in his office. He usually **8** ___ some Chinese food from a 'take-away' or a hamburger from a fast-food place.

When Steve was younger, he wanted to **9** ___ a job with an airline. He wanted to travel all over the world. He's going to retire in a few years and when he does, he may **10** ___ his own business.

B   Here are the ten missing words. Which gaps do they fill?

> down   up   get   get   get   start   take   gets
> gets   gets

C   Find out how many differences there are between Steve Ferrante and your partners.

> Do you live in a small house near Golden Gate Bridge?

> No, I live in a . . . near . . .

8 📢 LISTENING

A You are going to hear a telephone conversation between Booker Tucker (T), the head of security at GCS, and Sergeant Kovalski (K). Someone else is mentioned whose last name begins with 'H'. Listen and then tick (✓) the initial of the person who is going to do the things.

1 Who is going to watch some videotapes tomorrow?

T ☐ K ✓ H ☐

2 Who is going to make the necessary arrangements?

T ☐ K ☐ H ☐

3 Who is going to the place where the other person works?

T ☐ K ☐ H ☐

4 Who asks the other person to repeat some important information?

T ☐ K ☐ H ☐

5 Who will give more information if necessary?

T ☐ K ☐ H ☐

6 Who is going to leave work around 4 o'clock tomorrow afternoon?

T ☐ K ☐ H ☐

7 Who is going to change his or her plans for tomorrow?

T ☐ K ☐ H ☐

B 👥 Now complete the questions below. Then ask your partner the complete questions.

1 What is Sergeant Kovalski ___ to do tomorrow?
2 Will Mr Tucker ___ there?
3 Who ___ assistant head ___ security at GCS?
4 Why is ___ going to change ___ plans?

9 USEFUL TELEPHONE LANGUAGE

A Here are some phrases you have just heard. Connect the two parts of each phrase.

1	Sorry to bother	A	arrange that for me?
2	It's about the	B	very helpful.
3	I'm with you	C	you again.
4	Could you	D	just fine.
5	Just one more	E	to help.
6	Could you make	F	it a bit earlier?
7	That sounds	G	tapes you mentioned.
8	You've been	H	now.
9	Always glad	I	thing.

B Now repeat the complete phrase that you think means the following.

1 I didn't understand you before but I do now.
2 Can you come a little sooner than that?
3 I'm sure that will be all right.
4 Thank you for your information or service.
5 Don't put the phone down yet. This won't take long.
6 I'm calling you in regard to the following thing which we have spoken about before.
7 Will you please do whatever is necessary so that I can do what I want to do?
8 Please contact me again if you need information or something else.
9 I hope you won't mind if I ask you to do something more for me.

10 📢 PRONUNCIATION

A Listen and repeat. Notice how the pronunciation of the words 'to', 'for', 'at', 'them', 'him' and 'can', change in ordinary, everday speech.

1 (*to*) Sorry to bother you again.
2 (*for*) Ask for Andy Hewitt.
3 (*at*) No problem at all, Sergeant.
4 (*them*) Do you want me to send them over to you?
5 (*him*) If you want to talk to him, you should be here before four.
6 (*can*) If you have any questions, he can answer them.

13 CAN I BE FRANK?

1 👥 TALK ABOUT IT

1 Describe the woman in the picture. What is she wearing? How old do you think she is?
2 What do you think Robert and the woman are talking about?

2 🔊 CONVERSATION

DAY 6 : SATURDAY : 3.00 P.M. : COFFEE-SHOP

SILVINA   Why do you want my advice about the project?

ROBERT   Because you're an independent consultant who knows the company well. So you can be more objective than someone inside the company.

SILVINA   But I'm very busy at the moment.

ROBERT   We realize that. That's why I've been authorized to offer you $50,000 plus all expenses for the next ten days. Starting tomorrow.

SILVINA   Hmm. And in return you want me to act as a special consultant again.

ROBERT   Exactly. Well, what about it? Do you accept our offer?

SILVINA   Do you mind if I ask you a few questions before I answer that?

ROBERT   Of course not. Go ahead.

SILVINA   Who would I work with? Who would I give this advice to?

ROBERT   To me, of course.

SILVINA   Not to the Technical Director?

ROBERT   No. Why?

SILVINA   Can I be frank?

ROBERT   Of course.

SILVINA   Ed Bondy is a brilliant engineer. But it would be very difficult for me to work with him again . . . and probably just as difficult for him to work with me.

ROBERT   May I ask why?

SILVINA   Well, . . . uh . . . he and I have had some very serious disagreements.

ROBERT   About what?

👥 **Study these questions. How many can you and your partner answer?**

1 What exactly is 'the offer' that Robert talks about?
2 What will Silvina get if she says 'Yes' to this offer?
3 Who do you think 'authorized' Robert to make the offer?
4 Do you think Silvina would be happy to work with Ed Bondy again? Give reasons for your answer.
5 Describe some of the things Silvina will probably do in the next ten days.

3 WORDS & MEANINGS

A Study these definitions or meanings. What is the word that you think matches each meaning or definition? Some – but not all – of the words are in the conversation in Exercise 2.

1   Someone who does not work directly for a company but who is paid by the company to help them solve certain problems.
2   Something you give someone when you tell them what you think is the best thing for them to do.
3   Something you do when you say what someone should do.
4   Something you can also say about a country that has its own government and is not controlled by another country.
5   Money that a company pays to you for travel, hotel rooms, etc.
6   To give someone permission or power to do certain things for the company or in a job.
7   A way of saying 'Can I say what I really think?' (more than one word)

B What is the word you need to complete each of the following sentences?

1   Listen to my problem and then ___ me what to do about it.
2   Could you give me some ___ about this problem?
3   Here is some money to cover your ___ while you're away on business for us.
4   Do you want my honest opinion? I mean, can I be ___?
5   India was once ruled by Britain, but it has been ___ since 1948.
6   If you need independent advice, you have to find a good independent ___.
7   Who said you could pay so much money for a consultant? I mean, who ___ you to do it?

4 FORM & MEANING

A [image] In which pairs of sentences is there an important difference of meaning? Which sentences mean more or less the same thing?

▼ GRAMMAR 17A–B, p. 121
1 A   It would be difficult for Silvina to work with Ed Bondy again.
   B   It will be difficult for Silvina to work with Ed Bondy again.

▼ GRAMMAR 17C, p. 121
2 A   If I were her, I wouldn't do it.
   B   I don't think she should do it.

3 A   It would be bad if Bondy knew about it.
   B   It's good that Bondy doesn't know about it.

▼ GRAMMAR 18A–B, p. 121
4 A   He'll be angry when he hears about this.
   B   He'd be angry if he heard about this.

B Read aloud the sentences above that mean the following things.

A   Someone is going to tell Bondy about this and he is going to be very angry.
B   Silvina is going to work with Ed Bondy again and this is going to be difficult for her.
C   Silvina is not planning to work with Ed Bondy again. She knows how difficult it is.
D   He doesn't know about this. That's why he isn't angry.

C Say the correct words to complete each sentence.

1   Why would it be difficult if Silvina ___ with Ed Bondy again?
    A will work   B worked   C work

2   What ___ Bondy do if he knew about this offer?
    A would   B did   C does

3   If you were Silvina, ___ you accept the offer?
    A did   B do   C would

4   Why wouldn't you do it if you ___ her?
    A were   B would be   C are

5   If someone ___ you $50,000 for ten days work plus expenses, would you accept?
    A will offer   B would offer   C offered

5 READ & TALK ABOUT IT

A First, read this text about Andrea Dare, the woman Ed Bondy spoke to on the phone in Unit 11. Some words (1–13) are missing. What do you think they are?

Andrea Dare has her own company. It is **1** ___ 'Daring Solutions'. She lives **2** ___ the top of a very tall building with a wonderful view **3** ___ the city.

Her office isn't far away **4** ___ her apartment so she walks to work if the weather is fine. Andrea doesn't have a car and **5** ___ never learned to drive.

'I've **6** ___ about twenty boyfriends and four husbands so far. They all knew **7** ___ to drive. I would never **8** ___ time with a man if he didn't know how to drive. What else are men for?' she once **9** ___ a friend.

When it rains, as it often does in Portland, Andrea **10** ___ a taxi to her office. She hates getting wet. She **11** ___ at least $400 a week on taxis. She spends even more money every week **12** ___ restaurants. She likes good food, but she doesn't like cooking.

Andrea earns a lot of money. She likes spending it, but money isn't the most important thing in her life. Her work is. She works at **13** ___ twelve hours a day.

B Here are the missing thirteen words. Which gaps do they fill?

> spend   spends   how   called   least   of
> from   at   in   has   had   told   takes

C 👥 Tell your partner the differences you think there are between him or her and Andrea. Your partner will tell you if you are right or wrong.

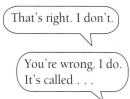

I don't think you have your own company.

That's right. I don't.

You're wrong. I do. It's called . . .

6 QUICK REVISION

A Explain the difference in meaning between the two sentences in each pair.

▼ GRAMMAR 16D, p. 120

1 A   I like living on the top floor of a very tall building.
  B   I'd like to live on the top floor of a very tall building.

2 A   I wouldn't like to work twelve hours a day.
  B   I don't like working twelve hours a day.

▼ GRAMMAR 17C, p. 121

3 A   When I was rich, I spent a lot of money on food.
  B   If I were rich, I'd spend a lot of money on food.

4 A   If I earned more, life would be easier.
  B   When I earned more, life was easier.

Which sentences above can you use:

- when the things you say in them are true; that is, things you do or did?

- for things or situations that aren't real, but are things or situations you imagine?

B Connect the two parts of each question.

1   What would you like to do if
2   What do you like
3   What would be different about your life
4   What was different about your life

A   if you were ten years younger?
B   when you were ten years younger?
C   doing when you have a lot of free time?
D   you had a lot of money?

C 👥 Now ask your partners the complete questions in Exercise B.

D 👥 How many of these sentences can you and your partners complete?

- If I had a lot more money, the first thing I would buy would be . . .

- If someone with a lot of money wanted to marry me but I didn't love that person, I would . . .

- If I knew I had only six months to live, I'd . . .

7 STRESS & PRONUNCIATION

A 🔊 **Say the pairs of words with your teacher or as you listen to the recording. Notice that the words on the left have stress on the first syllable and the words on the right have stress on the second syllable. None of the words is stressed on the third syllable.**

1	<u>won</u>-der-ful	im-<u>por</u>-tant
2	<u>ham</u>-burg-er	con-<u>sul</u>-tant
3	<u>di</u>-ffer-ent	o-<u>pin</u>-ion
4	<u>gov</u>-ern-ment	im-<u>press</u>-ion
5	<u>tel</u>-e-phone	a-<u>ppoint</u>-ment

B **Now say the pairs of words below. The stress for both words in each pair is on the same syllable. Is the stress on the first or the second syllable?**

1	important	consultant
2	expensive	computer
3	different	telephone
4	brilliant	exercise
5	expensive	solution
6	probably	authorize
7	difficult	visitors
8	impressive	arrangement
9	sarcastic	opinion

🔊 **Now listen to the words.**

C **Now look at these groups of words. In each group there are three words. One of the three words has the stress on a different syllable. Say the different word.**

EXAMPLE different   expensive   computer
ANSWER different
        (<u>di</u>-ffer-ent   ex-<u>pen</u>-sive   com-<u>put</u>-er)

1	probably	different	solution
2	different	government	appointment
3	brilliant	telephone	arrangement
4	expensive	different	hamburger
5	impressive	wonderful	telephone

🔊 **Now listen to the words.**

8 🔊 LISTENING

A **Robert and Silvina are talking. The first part of their conversation is almost the same as the version in Exercise 2 on page 56. However, there are *three* important differences. Listen at least once, then answer these questions.**

1 Why does Robert want Silvina's advice?
2 How much money does he offer her?
3 If she accepts the offer, when will she begin earning that money?
4 Who will she work with if she accepts it?

Which three questions above are about the important differences between what you read on page 56 and what you have just heard?

B **Listen to the second part of the conversation. Tick (✓) the best answer, A, B or C.**

1 What was the first thing Silvina and Ed Bondy disagreed about?

   A Who will buy the new version of RAINBOW? ☐
   B How many new things should it do? ☐
   C How much will customers pay for it? ☐

2 What exactly are the new things she thinks the new version of RAINBOW should do?

   A She doesn't say. ☐
   B It should be easy to use. ☐
   C It should be far more powerful. ☐

3 What was the other thing Silvina and Ed Bondy disagreed about?

   A Should the new version of RAINBOW be cheaper than the old version? ☐
   B Should the new version be more powerful than the old version? ☐
   C Should the new version be more powerful than the old version but just as easy to use? ☐

4 What is the important decision Silvina makes?

   A To go back to Argentina as soon as possible. ☐
   B To work directly with Robert as a consultant. ☐
   C To help Robert and the company to find another independent consultant. ☐

14 ARE YOU INTERESTED NOW?

1 🔊 READING

DAY 6 : SATURDAY : LATE AFTERNOON : SFPD

Lieutenant Ferrante walked into the large office where all the detectives worked. He looked worried.

'Have you seen Kovalski?' he asked.

'She's downstairs, watching a video. She got it from the company where that guy Hellman jumped out of a window the other day,' one of the detectives said.

'She's spending too much time on that case. All right. There are some strange things about it. But people often do all sorts of strange things before they kill themselves,' Ferrante thought as he walked down the stairs.

Kovalski was sitting in front of a video machine in a small room.

'I hear you've been watching a video,' he said.

'Yes, that's right. I think you should watch it, too.'

She turned the machine on. Two men were standing in front of an elevator. They were wearing brown uniforms with the name of a well-known security company on them.

'So, what's so interesting about this?' Ferrante asked.

'Just watch. You'll be surprised.'

The two men got into the elevator. One of them was carrying a small package.

'Two men in an elevator. Really fascinating,' Ferrante said. But he didn't sound interested at all.

'This happened a few minutes before Hellman fell out of the window. One of these men told the receptionist that they wanted to deliver something to someone on the fifteenth floor. Hellman's office was on the sixteenth floor. Now watch this,' Kovalski told him.

She ejected the cassette, and put another one in the machine. The scene changed. One of the men in uniform was giving the small package to a man in an office.

'What happened to the other guy?' Ferrante asked.

'I don't know, Steve. But as you can see, he wasn't there when the package was delivered. And remember. Hellman was on the next floor.'

Ferrante stared at her.

'Are you interested now?' she asked.

2 TALK ABOUT IT

👤👤 **Discuss these three questions.**

1 Where did Kovalski get the videotapes?
2 Why did Kovalski want Ferrante to watch them?
3 What do you think could have happened to the second man who got into the elevator? Where could he have gone? What could he have done?

3 FORM & MEANING

A 👤👤 Explain the difference in meaning.

1 A   What are you doing?
  B   What have you been doing?

2 A   Have you watched this video?
  B   Have you been watching this video?

3 A   Have you ever drunk wine?
  B   Have you been drinking wine?

B 👤👤 Match the questions with these possible answers.

A   Yes, once or twice. But I prefer beer.
B   Watching this video. I finished a few minutes ago.
C   Watching this video. Can't you see?
D   Yes. I watched it yesterday. It's very interesting.
E   Yes, we have. We've almost finished.
F   Yes. Can you smell it on my breath?

C Now complete the sentences below, using the correct form of the verb in brackets ( ).

EXAMPLE
(learn)   I've *been learning* English for several years now and I still make mistakes.

1 (learn)   Here are some new words I ___ a few days ago.
2 (see)   ___ you ever ___ the film 'Casablanca'?
3 (drink)   You ___ whiskey. I can smell it on your breath.
4 (rain)   The streets are wet. Do you think it ___?
5 (rain)   This has been a very wet month. It ___ almost every day.
6 (rain)   It ___ for a few hours yesterday, and then it stopped.

4 QUICK REVISION

A Divide the sentences below into two groups.

GROUP A is for things that are still going on or that finished a very short time ago.

GROUP B is for things that are entirely in the past – that is, we may not know when they finished but we can be sure they are definitely over.

▼ GRAMMAR 2 & 3, pp. 113–114
1   Kovalski has been working very hard on the Hellman case.
2   Tom Hellman worked very hard on RAINBOW.
3   Silvina Arcante worked on THE RAINBOW PROJECT, too, in its early stages.
4   She lived in San Francisco for five years.
5   She studied in San Francisco for four years.
6   She has been living in Buenos Aires for about eighteen months.
7   Have you been doing this exercise?
8   Have you done it yet?

B 👤👤 Match the two parts of each question. Then ask your partners the questions.

1   How many cups of tea or coffee do
2   How many cups have
3   How many cups did
4   How long have you been
5   How long did you
6   How many new words do you think you have
7   Did you

A   you drink yesterday?
B   spend studying English yesterday?
C   learnt today?
D   you usually drink every day?
E   learning English?
F   learn any new words yesterday?
G   you drunk today?

5 VOCABULARY PRACTICE

A 👥 **For each word in column A, there is a word in column B that is 'one step more'. What is that word?**

EXAMPLES good ▶ wonderful
           bad   ▶ terrible

A	B
good	bizarre
bad	impossible
warm	over-worked
dirty	huge
cold	wonderful
interesting	hot
strange	wet
tired	astonished
surprised	filthy
well-known	probably
difficult	fascinating
intelligent	famous
big	brilliant
busy	exhausted
possibly	freezing
damp	terrible

B **Now complete each sentence with a word from column A or B above.**

1 Yesterday it was cold but today it's worse; it's ___.
2 They say that Ed Bondy is more than intelligent; he's ___.
3 I wouldn't say I'm exhausted, but I am a little ___.
4 San Francisco is a big city, but Los Angeles is ___.
5 I don't think this story is really bizarre, but it is a little ___.
6 I'm more than surprised; I'm ___.
7 Are you saying that Hellman was possibly murdered or that he was ___ murdered?
8 This story isn't just interesting; it's ___.
9 What you're saying is more than just difficult to believe. It's ___ to believe!
10 The author of this book isn't really famous, however he is ___.
11 You said you had some bad news, but it's worse than that. It's ___.

6 PRONUNCIATION

A **The verbs below are all irregular. In many (but not all) irregular verbs, the vowel sound changes for the past tense. For example:**

PRESENT	PAST
come/comes	came
eat/eats	ate

🔊 **Now look at these verbs. The letters for the vowel sounds do not always change. However, sometimes the pronunciation does. Tick (✓) all the verbs that you think change in this way.**

PRESENT	PAST	
deal	dealt	✔
build	built	☐
learn	learnt	☐
hear	heard	☐
have	had	☐
lose	lost	☐
make	made	☐
mean	meant	☐
pay	paid	☐
say	said	☐
read	read	☐

B 🔊 **Now say the four words in each group. The vowel sound of one word in each group is different. Which word is it?**

EXAMPLE heard bird word hear
ANSWER   hear

1 lose   lost   cost   boss
2 pay   say   paid   said
3 mean   meant seen   leave
4 hear   heard near   here
5 meant went   sent   means
6 quick build built will

C **Now say the sentences below. The sound of 'ea' in 'read' changes only once. When?**

1 Do you read a newspaper?
2 Yes, sometimes I read 'The Post' and sometimes I read 'The Times'.
3 Which one are you reading now?
4 'The Post', but yesterday I read 'The Times'.

7))) LISTENING

A 👥 **Before you listen, look at the pictures. One of the objects is a hypodermic needle. The other is a spray. Answer these questions.**

1   What are hypodermic needles used for?
2   Who uses them?
3   Do you ever use a spray? If so, why, and what for?
4   If someone pushed Hellman out of the window of his office, why would that person probably use a needle or spray first?

B   Now listen to the complete conversation between Kovalski and Ferrante. There is some new information in the conversation. Then answer these questions.

1   What do you think Ferrante really wants to talk about before Kovalski shows him the videotapes?
2   Kovalski has looked at the videotape from cameras on the *first* and *fifteenth* floor. Why hasn't she looked at a videotape from the camera on the *sixteenth* floor?
3   What does Kovalski think really happened on Monday morning, around 10.55?
4   Why does she think that the person responsible for Hellman's death is someone inside the company?
5   There is a very important question she still can't answer. What is that question?

C 👥 **Discuss the questions below.**

■   Describe what the killer probably did from the time he entered the building on Monday to the time he left.

■   The person who paid the killer must have had a motive. What do you think that motive could have been?

8 TALKING ABOUT TIME

A   First, choose the best way to complete each question; A, B, C or D.

1   How long ___ to do an exercise like this?

A   does it need you   c   does it take you
B   do you spend   D   does it need for you

2   How much time ___ every day studying English?

A   are you taking   c   do you need
B   do you take   D   do you spend

3   How long does a typical English lesson ___?

A   last   c   takes
B   spend   D   need

B 👤 **Now ask your partners the questions above.**

C   Now match the parts of each question.

1   Did it
2   How much time did you spend
3   How long do you think it usually
4   How much longer is this lesson
5   Do you need any more time

A   to finish this exercise?
B   take you very long to do the last exercise?
C   going to last?
D   studying English yesterday?
E   takes to learn a foreign language well?

D 👥 **Talk about these questions with your partners.**

■   Where are you going after this lesson? How long will it take you to get there?

■   What are two or three things you do every morning after you get up? How long does it take you to do them?

■   How much time do you usually spend every day:
    • reading a newspaper
    • travelling
    • shopping
    • talking on the phone

■   What else do you often spend more than half an hour doing?

15 CUSTOMERS ALWAYS COMPLAIN

1 👥 TALK ABOUT THE PICTURE

1 Tell your partners everything you know about the three men.
2 Which man is the Technical Director on THE RAINBOW PROJECT?
3 Which man is the boss of GCS?
4 What do you think they are talking about?

2 🔊 CONVERSATION

DAY 7 : SUNDAY : A.M. : CRISIS MEETING : LARRY KNOWLES' OFFICE : GCS

ROBERT   A lot of customers are complaining about RAINBOW 3. They say it isn't as user-friendly as RAINBOW 2.

BONDY   Of course some customers are complaining. Customers always complain.

ROBERT   You mean it doesn't matter if they complain? Is that what you're saying?

BONDY   No, I'm saying that RAINBOW 3 isn't just a new version of RAINBOW 2. In many ways, it's a completely new product. It can do a lot of things RAINBOW 2 couldn't do. That's why it seems difficult to use.

ROBERT   Why do you say it 'seems' difficult to use? It *is* more difficult to use.

BONDY   No, it isn't. You'd understand that if you were an engineer.

ROBERT   The customers who are complaining aren't engineers, either. Are you telling me that their opinions are worthless?

BONDY   No, I'm trying to tell you that RAINBOW 3 has a lot of new features that RAINBOW 2 didn't have. The customers you're talking about simply aren't used to those new features yet. It takes time to get used to any new product or service. RAINBOW 3 is just as user-friendly as RAINBOW 2. Customers will realize that when they're more familiar with it.

ROBERT   But . . . if RAINBOW 3 is really as user-friendly as RAINBOW 2, why does it take so much more time to learn how to use it?

BONDY   It's a technical matter. If I had more time, I'd explain it to you. But even if I did, you probably wouldn't understand.

3 COMPREHENSION CHECK

**A Which explanations do you agree with?
Correct the explanations you disagree with.**

1 People *complain* when they are happy about
   something.
2 When people say 'it doesn't matter', they mean 'it
   doesn't work'.
3 A person's or a thing's *features* are those things
   that make that person or thing different from
   other people or things.
4 A computer is a *service* and advice about how to
   use it is a *product*.
5 If you have often seen someone's face before, it
   isn't a *familiar* face.
6 If you have never seen or done something before,
   you aren't *used to* it.

**B Work with someone else. Discuss
answers to these questions.**

1 Why are some customers unhappy?
2 Do you think Ed Bondy is very worried about
   these customers? Give reasons for your answer.
3 What does Ed Bondy think will happen after the
   customers get used to the new software?
4 What does Robert want Bondy to explain?
5 Why isn't Bondy going to explain it?

4 TALK ABOUT IT

**Choose at least one question and discuss it
with a partner.**

■ There are many Europeans and people from
   North and Central America visiting or living in
   Japan today. What things do you think they find
   difficult to get used to? Why is it difficult for them
   to get used to them?

■ Suppose you had to live in a foreign country for a
   year or so – for example, somewhere in Africa.
   What would you find difficult to get used to?

■ Think of something you have found difficult to
   get used to. What was it? Why was it difficult to
   get used to it? How long did it take you to get
   used to it?

5 FORM & MEANING

A What's the difference in meaning?

▼ GRAMMAR 16, 17 & 18, pp. 120–121

1 A If Ed had more time, he'd explain it to Robert.
  B If Ed has more time, he'll explain it to Robert.

2 A If Robert is an engineer, he'll understand.
  B If Robert were an engineer, he would
     understand.

3 A Will he understand when Ed explains it?
  B Will he understand if Ed explains it?

**B Which sentences above mean the
following things?**

A Ed is going to explain it to him, but will he
   understand it then?
B Robert won't understand because he isn't an
   engineer.
C Ed is not going to explain it because he doesn't
   have enough time.
D Perhaps Ed will have more time, and then he will
   explain it to Robert.
E If it is true that Robert really is an engineer, he
   will understand.
F It is possible but not certain that Ed will explain it
   to him, but will Robert understand even then?

C Match the two parts of each sentence.

1 What would you do if
2 What is the first thing you will do
3 Will you buy a new car next year
4 Would you buy a new car now
5 Where will you go when
6 What will you do tomorrow if

A this lesson ends?
B when you wake up tomorrow morning?
C you don't feel very well?
D you were rich?
E if you had enough money?
F if you have enough money?

**D Now ask your partner the six complete
questions in Exercise C.**

6 GRAMMAR

A What is the missing word in each sentence?

▼ GRAMMAR 17 &18, p. 121

1 What ___ you do if you had more money?
2 What ___ you do tomorrow if it rains?
3 If I ___ more time and money, my life would be a
   lot easier.
4 If the weather ___ better tomorrow, I'll go for a
   long walk.
5 I'll come and see you tomorrow if I ___ time.
6 I'd come and see you more often if I ___ more
   time.
7 English ___ be easier to learn if spelling and
   pronunciation were the same.
8 ___ you study tomorrow if you have time?

B Complete the following questions. Then ask your partner the complete questions.

A How ___ you feel tomorrow morning if you get
   only three hours sleep tonight?

B What would probably happen if you ___ only
   three hours sleep every night?

7 VOCABULARY REVISION

**Complete the sentences below,
using 'explain', 'say',
'talk' or 'tell'.**

1 What did Robert want to ___ to Ed about?
2 What did Ed ___ Robert about RAINBOW 3?
3 What did Ed ___ about RAINBOW 3?
4 Can you ___ the meaning of 'get used to' to me?
5 If you don't understand, please ___ me.
6 If you don't understand something, please ___ so.
7 Is there a word you would like me to ___?
8 Now, let's ___ about something else.

8 READ & TALK ABOUT IT

A Robert Keller talks about two different things he bought. Connect the two parts of each sentence.

EXAMPLE About four months ago, I saw   [E]

1 I went to a shop and had   ☐
2 I liked what I saw and so I   ☐
3 I'm very satisfied with it because   ☐
4 However, about a month ago I bought
   some software that I'm not   ☐
5 It isn't easy to use and it   ☐
6 I've complained about it and   ☐
7 But the people I bought it from say that
   all their other customers are   ☐
8 I'm glad I bought the new computer but   ☐

A tried to get my money back.
B it's much faster than the computer I used before.
C I wish I hadn't bought the software.
D very satisfied with it.
E an advertisement for a new computer.
F satisfied with at all.
G a look at it.
H doesn't run well on my computer, either.
I decided to buy it.

B Now talk about these questions with a partner.

1 What is Robert satisfied with?
2 What is he not satisfied with?
3 Why is he satisfied with one of the things and not
   satisfied with the other?

C Now tell your partners about something you are satisfied with – or something you aren't satisfied with. Be sure to answer these questions.

■ When did you begin using it?

■ What is good or bad about it?

■ If you aren't satisfied, what have you done
   about it?

9))) LISTENING

A This is the rest of the conversation that begins on page 64. Fifteen words (1–15) are missing. What do you think they are?

LARRY   I think what Ed is saying, Robert, is we usually get a few complaints from a few customers when we **1** ___ out a new product.

ROBERT   But these are more than a few complaints – and more than a few customers have **2** ___ them.

BONDY   Listen! Before we began developing RAINBOW 3, we asked customers all over the world what they wanted. And they all **3** ___ us the same thing. They want something far more powerful than RAINBOW 2. And that's what we've **4** ___ them.

ROBERT   But now that they have it, they aren't **5** ___ with it.

BONDY   I don't have time to **6** ___ with you. But before I leave, there's something I want to ask you.

ROBERT   What?

BONDY   I **7** ___ that when you came in this morning, Silvina Arcante was with you. Why?

ROBERT   I've **8** ___ her to help me.

BONDY   Help you? What do you **9** ___? How?

LARRY   As you say, Ed, Robert is not an engineer, and I know you don't have enough time to explain certain . . . technical **10** ___ to him. That's why I've **11** ___ Robert to employ Silvina as an independent consultant for a week or **12** ___.

BONDY   Well, if you want to throw the company's money away, I can't stop you! But just **13** ___ her away from me! And now, if you don't **14** ___, I have work to **15** ___!

B Now listen to the complete conversation and check.

10))) PRONUNCIATION

A When does the sound of the underlined letter or letters change?

1   surpri<u>s</u>e   surpri<u>s</u>ed   advi<u>s</u>e   advi<u>c</u>e
2   discu<u>ss</u>   discu<u>ss</u>ion   explana<u>ti</u>on   <u>s</u>he
3   <u>s</u>he   ma<u>ch</u>ine   <u>ch</u>oose   <u>s</u>hoes
4   s<u>t</u>udy   fea<u>t</u>ure   wa<u>tch</u>   <u>ch</u>ip

B Say the following sentences aloud. Which words have the following sounds?

1   'se' in house
2   'sh' in she
3   'z' in zero
4   'ch' in Chinese

A   How many customers are using these machines?
B   Watch this demonstration of these new features.
C   Most new users realize how useful these features are when they get used to them.
D   You used to use a surprising mixture of these chips.

11 VOCABULARY REVISION ('DO' OR 'MAKE')

Complete the sentences. Use the correct words from the boxes.

do does did done doing	make made making

1   A lot of customers have ___ complaints about this product.
2   What are you going to ___ about these complaints?
3   We've already ___ everything we can.
4   Ed Bondy always ___ the same thing when a customer complains.
5   What's he ___ now? I mean, is he busy?
6   I think he's ___ a phone call, so don't disturb him.
7   Kovalski thinks Tom Hellman was murdered, and wants to find out who ___ it.
8   She thinks that someone ___ at least one serious mistake a few days ago.
9   She thinks they will ___ another mistake soon.

16 JUST A COINCIDENCE?

1 👥 TALK ABOUT THE PICTURE

1 Who is the woman in Robert's office?
2 Tell your partners everything you can remember about her.

2 🔊 READING

DAY 7 : SUNDAY A.M. : ROBERT'S OFFICE : GCS

Silvina was working with RAINBOW 3 when Robert came back from the crisis meeting. He went to the window and looked out.

'Have you ever heard of a company called DS, in Portland, Oregon?' Silvina suddenly asked.

Robert turned around and stared at her. 'Yes. Why?'

'Well, perhaps I should have mentioned this before, but I didn't think it was so important. There's an American company in Buenos Aires that's trying out one of their programs. It's a test version of a software program called DARING. I had a close look at the program last month. And now that I've had a chance to look at RAINBOW again, I'm . . . well . . . surprised.'

'Why are you surprised?' Robert asked.

'Many of the important features are very similar. In fact they're almost identical.'

'But how is that possible?'

'Well, it may just be a coincidence, but somehow I doubt that. I mean, there must be another explanation,' Silvina answered.

She stopped and looked at Robert.

'Yes, go on, Silvina. What do you think that explanation could be?' he said.

'Someone in this company may be giving DS information about RAINBOW,' she said in a very low voice.

👥 **How many of these questions can you and your partner answer?**

1 How do you think Robert felt when he came back from the crisis meeting with Ed Bondy and Larry Knowles?
2 Why do you think Robert 'turned around and stared' when Silvina mentioned a company in Portland?
3 What exactly does Silvina find surprising about the DARING software program?
4 What do you think is the most surprising thing that Silvina says to Robert?
5 Look at the last thing Silvina says. Then explain why you think she says it in 'a very low voice'.

3 WORDS & MEANINGS

**Find the words or phrases in the text in
Exercise 2 that mean the following things.**

1 What you do when you test something by
using it.
2 What you do when you inspect or examine
something carefully.
3 What you can say about two or more things that
look almost the same.
4 What you can say about two or more things that
look exactly the same.
5 Two or more things that are not planned but
which are surprising because they happen at the
same time.
6 To think that perhaps something is not possible or
right.

4 TALK ABOUT IT

Discuss at least one question.

■ If someone is giving important information to the
company called 'DS', who do you think it could
be? Explain why you think it could be this person.

■ What do you think that person's motive could be?

■ If Silvina is right, what should she and Robert do?

■ Suppose you worked in an international company
and you think that someone you work with – a
friend perhaps – is selling important information
to a competitor. What would you do?

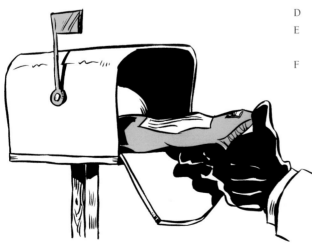

5 FORM & MEANING

A **Study the six pairs of sentences. Which
pairs do you think mean more or less the
same thing? When is there an important
difference in meaning? Can you explain to
your partners what that difference is?**

▼ GRAMMAR 20B, p. 122; 21A–B, p. 123
1 A Perhaps this is just a coincidence.
  B This may be just a coincidence.

2 A There's something I should tell you.
  B There's something I should have told you.

▼ GRAMMAR 20B–C, p. 122
3 A There must be an explanation.
  B There should be an explanation.

4 A You should tell Larry about this.
  B You must tell Larry about this.

5 A San Francisco must be very interesting.
  B I've never been to San Francisco, but from what
   I've heard, I'm sure it's a very interesting city.

▼ GRAMMAR 22A, p. 123
6 A Someone may give information to 'DS'.
  B Someone may be giving information to 'DS'.

B **Which sentences above mean the
following things. Remember that sometimes
two sentences can have the same meaning.**

A It is possible that someone will give information
to 'DS'.
B Tell Larry about this!
C I'm sure there is an explanation but I don't know
what it is.
D I'm sorry I didn't tell you about this before.
E It is possible that someone has already given
information to 'DS' and will do so again.
F My advice to you is tell Larry about this. That's
probably the best thing to do.

6 GRAMMAR & VOCABULARY REVISION

Say the correct words to complete each sentence.

1 Silvina should ___ Robert about this earlier, but she didn't.
   A has told   B have told   C tell

2 What do you mean you should have told me about this? Why ___ you?
   A haven't   B don't   C didn't

3 I can't believe that someone in this company has given ___ information to one of our competitors.
   A an important   B a important   C important

4 Who would ___ such a thing?
   A do   B make   C give

5 Can you explain ___?
   A me that   B that to me   C me about that

6 Could it be the same person who ___ Tom Hellman a few days ago?
   A has killed   B was killing   C killed

7 Let me give you ___ advice.
   A a   B an   C some

8 In my opinion, we ___ contact the police immediately.
   A will   B would   C should

9 It will be better if we ___ this now and not later.
   A do   B will do   C would do

7 TALK ABOUT IT

Who is giving information to DS? Could it be one of these three people? If you think so, explain why. If you don't think so, also explain why. Talk about the possible motives of each person.

LARRY KNOWLES, the head of GCS. Larry's second wife wants a divorce and this will be very expensive.

ED BONDY, the Technical Director. He thinks he should be the head of the company but now realizes that will never be possible.

ROBERT KELLER, director of executive training. He is a psychologist, not an engineer. He and Ed Bondy do not have a good relationship.

8 FIVE DIFFERENT MEANINGS OF 'HAVE'

A   Study these five different meanings.

1 To possess or own something, or to be responsible for it in some way or other:
   (American English) *I have a car. Do you have a car?*
   (British English) *I've got a car. Have you got a car?*

2 To do or experience something:
   We're having a party tomorrow and hope you will come. Please have a good look at this. Are you having a good time?

3 Alternative to *must*:
   If this is true, we have to tell the police about it.

4 To cause something to be done:
   I'm going to have my hair cut tomorrow. Where can I have my car repaired?

5 Give birth to a baby:
   Mary is going to have a baby soon.

B   Here are some more examples. Which of the five meanings above does each example have? Give the number of that meaning.

EXAMPLE   You have to listen to this!   3

A   Larry has a beautiful house in Napa Valley.   ___
B   He is going to have another house built soon.   ___
C   Every morning he has a swim in his pool.   ___
D   Larry has a wife and a girlfriend.   ___
E   He is having a very bad time with his wife because she knows about the girlfriend.   ___
F   The girlfriend had a little girl recently.   ___
G   Larry has a very good job.   ___
H   He also has a lot of debts.   ___
I   He has to find more money in order to pay those debts.   ___
J   Is it possible that he had Hellman killed?   ___

9 ◗)) Listening

A Ed Bondy is talking to another man. Listen. Then choose the correct answer to the questions.

1 What is Ed doing?
   A Getting information at an airport.
   B Making a reservation.
   C Neither A nor B.

2 Why is Ed surprised?
   A Someone isn't there already.
   B Someone he doesn't know is waiting for him.
   C The other man doesn't know who he is.

3 Ed mentions a woman. Where is she?
   A In another room waiting for Ed.
   B We don't know exactly.
   C Probably in San Francisco.

4 What did the other man notice about the woman?
   A The way she spoke.
   B Something about her name.
   C Her English wasn't very good.

5 What did the other man think before Ed arrived?
   A That the woman would arrive before Ed.
   B That she would probably come later.
   C That she would not come at all.

6 What is the other man going to change?
   A The date of the reservation.
   B The amount of money Ed is going to pay.
   C The kind of room Ed will be staying in.

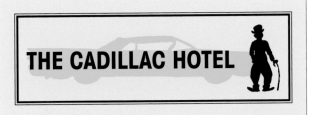

THE CADILLAC HOTEL

B Read these questions then listen again and answer them.

1 Where has Ed just come from?
2 Why did the woman speak to the other man?
3 What exactly did the other man notice when she spoke?
4 What do you think Ed is probably going to do after the other man returns his credit card?

10 Giving and getting advice

A 👤👤 You and a friend are talking about where to stay and where to eat. Read aloud your part below. Your partner has to find the friend's part (A–G) and read it aloud.

YOU   Have you ever been to Los Angeles?
FRIEND **0** _C_ . *Yes, several times. Why?*

YOU   Well, I'm going to spend a few days there next month. Can you recommend a hotel?
FRIEND **1** ___ .
YOU   I'm not sure yet, but I'd like to be as close to the ocean as possible.
FRIEND **2** ___ .
YOU   Is it very expensive?
FRIEND **3** ___ .
YOU   Have you got the telephone number?
FRIEND **4** ___ .
YOU   Of course. Oh, just two more questions. Are there any good restaurants near the hotel and how do I get there?
FRIEND **5** ___ .
YOU   How do I get there?
FRIEND **6** ___ .

A Yes, but not with me. Can I give it to you the next time I see you?
B That's easy. You can rent a car at the airport or get a mini-bus that will take you there for less than $20.
C Yes, several times. Why?
D Not really. It's good value for money.
E In that case, I'd recommend The Cadillac Hotel. It's right on Venice Beach, not too far from the airport.
F Well, the answer to the first question is yes, there are. Lots of them. What was the second question again?
G That depends. Which part of the city are you going to stay in?

B 👤👤 👤👤 Work in groups of three or four. Think of another place you would like to visit. Find out if anybody in the group has ever been there and if they can tell you where to stay and how to get there.

17 TWENTY-FOUR HOURS

1 👤👥 TALK ABOUT THE PICTURES

Which person in the pictures:

1 is a brilliant engineer?
2 drinks too much coffee and smokes a lot?
3 used to work for GCS until last Monday?

2 CONVERSATION

A 🔊 **Listen to the first part of the conversation.**

DAY 7 : SUNDAY : LATE AFTERNOON : SFPD

FERRANTE	I'm going to turn the case over to the FBI, Ros.
KOVALSKI	I need another twenty-four hours, Steve. Give me another twenty-four hours.
FERRANTE	You've already spent far too much time on this case.
KOVALSKI	I'm close, Steve. I'm very close.
FERRANTE	Close to what?
KOVALSKI	Close to finding out if Bondy hired the killer, and if he did, why he did it. That's why you have to give me another twenty-four hours.
FERRANTE	No, Ros. It'll save everybody's time if I turn the case over to the FBI now. If I don't, you'll never solve the other cases you're working on.
KOVALSKI	I'll never find out if Bondy did it unless you give me another day. Neither will the FBI.
FERRANTE	I need you for other cases.
KOVALSKI	Just another twenty-four hours. That's all I'm asking for. Something very important is going to happen in the next twenty-four hours.
FERRANTE	How can you be sure?
KOVALSKI	I think I understand now how Bondy's mind works. That's why I think he's going to do something in the next twenty-four hours that will help us to answer some very important questions.
FERRANTE	Which questions?

B 🔊 **Now listen to the complete conversation, which includes a second part.**

👤👥 **Then discuss these questions with your partners.**

1 What is the first question Kovalski wants to answer?
2 What is the second question she wants to answer?

3 COMPREHENSION CHECK

Find the words or phrases in the text in Exercise 2 that mean these things.

1 To give something you are responsible for to someone else who will then take responsibility for it.

2 Three letters that mean 'Federal Bureau of Investigation', the organization that deals with cases that involve national crimes in the United States.

3 One word which means 'If . . . not' or 'One thing will or should happen only if something else happens first'.

4 A phrase we use not for somebody's brain but for the way a person uses that brain.

5 What you do when you pay money so that someone will do something or so that you can use something.

4 👥 TALK ABOUT IT

■ Find out at least three things your partners are probably going to do in the next twenty-four hours.

■ Now complete the question below and then ask at least two people that question.
. . . you have to do anything . . . the next twenty-four hours that you would prefer not to . . . ?

■ If the answer to the question above is 'Yes', find out what the person who answered it has to do and why he or she has to do it.

■ Why is it so difficult to find out how someone's mind works? How can you find this out?

5 FORM & MEANING

A 👥 When is there an important difference in meaning?

▼ GRAMMAR 8 & 9, pp. 116–117

1 A What will happen in the next twenty-four hours?
  B What is going to happen in the next twenty-four hours?

2 A Will you have a baby?
  B Are you going to have a baby?

3 A Will you lend me some money?
  B Are you going to lend me some money?

▼ GRAMMAR 23A, p. 124

4 A What does Ferrante think will happen if he turns the case over to the FBI?
  B What does Ferrante think will happen unless he turns the case over to the FBI?

5 A What does Kovalski think will happen unless Ferrante gives her another day?
  B What does Kovalski think is going to happen if Ferrante doesn't give her another day?

B 👥 Here are some possible answers to the questions in Exercise A. Which questions do you think these answers go with? Remember that sometimes the same answer can go with more than one question.

A He is afraid Kovalski will never solve all the other cases she is working on.

B He thinks she'll have more time to spend on the other cases she's working on.

C She is afraid she'll never find out if Bondy had anything to do with Hellman's murder.

D Yes, in about eight months. How did you know?

E What a strange question. How can anybody possibly answer it?

C Now answer these questions.

1 Look at questions 3A and 3B in Exercise A again. Which question would you probably ask if you were talking to a friend and you needed some money?

2 Which question (3A or 3B) suggests that your friend already knows you want some money and you are waiting for a clear 'Yes' or 'No' answer?

6 GRAMMAR

A **Complete the sentences below. Sometimes two choices are possible.**

1 Do you think ___ tomorrow?
 A it's going to rain B it'll rain C it rains

2 The question people usually ask when they want to marry someone else is '___ marry me?'
 A Do you B Will you C Are you going to

3 I'm very tired and unless I ___ a good night's sleep tonight, I'll feel even more tired tomorrow.
 A don't get B won't get C get

4 I'm looking for a job. I just don't know what I'll do ___ find one soon.
 A when I B if I don't C unless I

5 If you want to use someone's pen, you can say 'Excuse me, do you mind ___ use your pen?'
 A me to B if I C that I

6 Another way of saying the same thing is '___ you lend me your pen, please?'
 A Will B Would C Are you going to

7 A young woman who got married a month ago often feels very strange in the morning. Perhaps she ___ a baby.
 A will have B is going to have C is having

8 Kovalski will never find out why Hellamn was killed ___ more time.
 A if she doesn't get B unless she gets
 C if she gets

B 👥 **Discuss with your partner what words you think are missing.**

Ed Bondy got on a plane to Los Angeles a few hours **1** ___. Now he's waiting **2** ___ a woman in a hotel on Venice Beach. She said she would be there before him, but she hasn't come **3** ___. He's already angry and he'll get even angrier **4** ___ she comes soon. In fact, he's so angry that **5** ___ she doesn't come soon, he'll probably become dangerous. But there's something he doesn't know. The woman is also very dangerous – much more dangerous **6** ___ Ed realizes. In other words, **7** ___ Ed is very careful, something very bad will happen to him. What do you think **8** ___ happen when they meet?

7 VOCABULARY PRACTICE

A 👥 **Match the phrases (1–10) with their opposites (A–J).**

1 Be frank!
2 Someone planned this.
3 Is this valuable?
4 She spoke in a low voice.
5 She got angry.
6 I've never seen it before.
7 She had a close look at it.
8 There must be an explanation for this.
9 It's fascinating.
10 You should turn this over to the FBI.

A No, it's worthless.
B Unless you solve it, nobody ever will.
C She didn't examine it.
D Don't tell me what you really think.
E How boring!
F It was a coincidence.
G We'll never know why this happened.
H It looks very familiar.
I She shouted.
J She stayed calm.

B **Now use words from the phrases above to complete each sentence.**

1 Have you ever seen this before? I mean, does it look ___?

2 Examine this carefully. In other words, take a very ___ ___ ___ it.

3 I don't think anybody planned this. It must have been ___ ___.

4 Sometimes your advice is very valuable but at other times it's absolutely ___.

5 Do you really want to know what I think? In other words, can I ___ ___?

6 Shh, someone may hear us, so please speak in a very ___ ___.

7 Kovalski is the only person who can solve this case. ___ she finds out why Hellman was killed, nobody ever will.

8 I'm sure we can find out why this happened. There ___ ___ ___ ___!

9 Some people think this story is boring, but others find it ___.

8 Pronunciation

A))) **How does the pronunciation of the underlined word change?**

1 A The hotel is <u>close</u> to the beach.
  B <u>Close</u> the door, please.

2 A Have you <u>used</u> a computer before?
  B I <u>used</u> to work in a bank.

3 A Please <u>read</u> this.
  B Have you <u>read</u> this before?

4 A I <u>read</u> this last week.
  B Did you <u>read</u> it last week, too?

5 A Let me see the <u>records</u>.
  B A tape recorder <u>records</u> sounds on tape.

6 A Where do you <u>live</u>?
  B This concert is coming to you <u>live</u>.

B Now answer these questions.

1 In which sentence in Exercise A does the word 'used' have the same sound as 'z' in 'zero'?
2 In which sentences is the word 'read' pronounced in the same way as 'red'?
3 When is the stress '<u>re</u>-cord'?
4 When is it 're-<u>cord</u>'?
5 Which underlined word has the same 'i' sound as in 'five'?
6 Which underlined word has the same 'i' sound as in 'six'?

C))) **Now read these pairs of sentences aloud. Do the underlined letters have the same or a different sound?**

1 A I don't <u>know</u> very much about this.
  B A little <u>know</u>ledge is a dangerous thing.

2 A Where is this bus <u>go</u>ing?
  B Has the bus <u>go</u>ne?

3 A What do you <u>do</u>?
  B What are you <u>do</u>ing?

4 A What does Bondy <u>do</u>?
  B What has Bondy <u>do</u>ne?

5 A I p<u>ai</u>d the bill yesterday
  B The customer s<u>ai</u>d he paid the bill.

9))) Listening

Listen to the rest of the conversation that begins on page 72. Which of the statements below are True (T)? Which are False (F)?

1 Kovalski thinks Hellman's murder was planned very carefully. ☐
2 Ferrante is surprised when Kovalski says this. ☐
3 Ferrante says that one small thing went wrong when Hellman was killed. ☐
4 Kovalski thinks that only a brilliant engineer like Bondy could have planned a murder so carefully. ☐
5 She thinks that someone else worked with Bondy in some way. ☐
6 Bondy was probably not thinking very clearly when the murder was planned. ☐
7 Kovalski doesn't think the FBI will ever be able to find the answers that she is looking for. ☐
8 At the end, Ferrante says something that shows he is going to turn the case over to the FBI immediately. ☐

10 Talk about it

👤👥 **Choose a question. Discuss it with your partner.**

■ Kovalski says 'Only a woman could have persuaded Bondy to take risks like that'. What kind of risks do you think she was talking about? Why does she say 'only a woman'?

■ When was the last time you took a risk? What was the risk and what happened?

■ What does Kovalski persuade Ferrante to do? What does she say or do that persuades him to do it?

18 THE OLD PIER

1 👥 TALK ABOUT THE PICTURES

1 What do you think Bondy has been doing since he arrived at the hotel?
2 Who do you think he is speaking to on the phone?

2 🔊 CONVERSATION

DAY 7 : SUNDAY : EVENING : THE CADILLAC HOTEL

ED BONDY IS IN THE HOTEL ON VENICE BEACH, CALIFORNIA. THE PHONE RANG JUST A FEW SECONDS AGO.

WOMAN It's me.
BONDY I've been waiting for you for an hour.
WOMAN I'm sorry, I really am.
BONDY Why aren't you here, damn it?
WOMAN Have you been drinking? Is that why you're shouting? Are you drunk?
BONDY I'm not shouting.
WOMAN Yes, you are.
BONDY And I'm not drunk, either.
WOMAN Then stop shouting.
BONDY Where the hell are you?
WOMAN Near the hotel.
BONDY Near the hotel? Why aren't you here?
WOMAN I'll explain later. Do you know where the old pier is?
BONDY Where the what is?
WOMAN The old pier. It's near the hotel. Walk out of the hotel, turn left and then walk along the beach for about ten minutes. You can't miss it.
BONDY I can't miss what? What are you talking about?
WOMAN The old pier. I'll wait for you there. I have something important to tell you. Hurry.
BONDY Why should I go there? Why don't you come here?
WOMAN I will. But not now. Later. I'll explain everything to you when you get there.
BONDY Explain it to me now.
WOMAN Stop arguing, Ed. I'm not going to say anything more until you come to the old pier.

👥 **Answer these questions about the conversation.**

1 Why is Bondy angry?
2 What does the woman want him to do?
3 What does he want her to do?
4 What do you think Ed is going to do after this conversation?

3 COMPREHENSION CHECK

Which explanations do you agree with? Correct the explanations you disagree with.

1   People ask questions like 'Why aren't you here, damn it?' and 'Where the hell are you?' when they are calm, not angry.

2   When the woman asks 'Have you been drinking?' she probably means drinking things like coffee, tea, coca-cola or perhaps milk.

3   When she says 'You can't miss it,' she means 'It's very easy to see and find.'

4   When people hurry, they go much slower than they usually do.

5   When the woman says 'I'm not going to say anything more until you come to the old pier,' she means that first he must go to the old pier and then she will say something more.

6   People argue when they have the same opinion about something.

4 TALK ABOUT IT

👤👤 **Choose at least two questions and discuss them with a partner. Remember that many answers are possible to the questions.**

■   Suppose you have arranged to meet someone at eight in the evening. It is now nine and that person still hasn't come. What would you probably do?

■   Have you ever been late for an appointment or meeting? If so, explain why you were late and what you did when you got to the appointment or meeting.

■   Why do you think the woman wants to talk to Ed at the old pier and not at the hotel?

5 FORM & MEANING

A 👤👤 **When is there an important difference in meaning?**

▼ GRAMMAR 3A–B, p. 114

1 A   Have you been drinking whiskey?

   B   Have you ever drunk whiskey?

▼ GRAMMAR 24B, p. 124; 25B, p. 125

2 A   You keep saying that.

   B   You say that again and again.

3 A   Stop shouting!

   B   Would you mind not shouting?

▼ GRAMMAR 18A–B, p. 121

4 A   I'll explain everything when you come to the old pier.

   B   I'll explain everything if you come to the old pier.

▼ GRAMMAR 23A–B, p. 124

5 A   I'm not going to say anything more unless you come to the old pier.

   B   I'm not going to say anything more until you come to the old pier.

B 👤👤 **Now answer these questions about the sentences in Exercise A.**

1   Which question (1A or 1B) could you give this answer to? 'Yes, once or twice, but not recently.'

2   Which two sentences:
   A   suggest very strongly that Andrea is sure that Ed will come to the old pier?
   B   suggest that perhaps Andrea is not absolutely sure that Ed will come to the old pier?

C 👤👤 **Talk about it**

1   Explain the difference in these sentences.
   A   The shops here are open at 9 o'clock.
   B   The shops here are open until 9 o'clock.

2   Which sentences below sound strange. Explain why they seem strange.
   A   The all-night party will go on until the sun rises.
   B   The all-night party will go on unless the sun rises.
   C   What will all the guests do if the sun comes up?
   D   What will all the guests do when the sun comes up?

6 TYPICAL RESPONSES

A Match the phrases and sentences (1–8) with their 'typical responses' or answers (A–H).

1 Hurry!
2 Are you in a hurry?
3 I've been waiting for you for an hour.
4 Listen. I have something important to tell you.
5 I'm very sorry.
6 Do you know where the station is?
7 How can I get there?
8 Are you drunk?

A Yes? What?
B Of course not. I'm completely sober.
C All right. I'll come as quickly as possible.
D You can walk. It isn't far.
E I'm sorry I'm so late.
F It's all right. Forget it.
G I'm afraid I don't. Sorry.
H No. I have a few minutes. Why?

B Here are some more typical responses to 1–8 in Exercise A. What is the phrase each 'response' is a possible answer to?

I Can you tell me later? I'm afraid I'm in a hurry.
J If I were you, I'd take a taxi. Just tell the driver where you want to go.
K There's no need to apologize. We all make mistakes sometimes.
L Why? What's the rush? Is there a fire or something?
M Yes, I'm afraid I am. Did you want to tell me something important?
N Yes. Turn left at the next corner. You'll see it in front of you. You can't miss it.
O I'm sorry. Didn't you get my message? I said I was going to be late.
P You know I never touch alcohol.

C ⚫ Work in pairs. One of you reads a phrase or sentence from 1–8 in Exercise A. If your partner can think of a good 'response', without looking at the book, then he/she reads from 1–8 aloud. If your partner can't think of a good response, you read another phrase or sentence from 1–8 aloud.

7 VOCABULARY PRACTICE

A Which word does not belong with the other three?

1 walk   run   hurry   rush
2 hurry   rush   fast   slow
3 shout   loud   angry   whisper
4 shout   low   quiet   whisper
5 drunk   coffee   alcohol   whiskey
6 hungry   food   eat   drink
7 eat   drink   thirsty   water
8 regret   sorry   apologize   thank

B Read these sentences aloud. When does the meaning of 'afraid' change?

1 I'm afraid I'll be a few minutes late.
2 I'm afraid I can't come.
3 I'm afraid of dogs but not cats.
4 I'm afraid I can't explain the difference.

C Complete the phrases below with 'afraid' or 'sorry'.

1 I can't help you. I'm very ___.
2 Some people are ___ to go out into the street late at night.
3 I'm ___ to tell you this but you're fired!
4 I'm ___ I have some bad news for you. You're fired!
5 I'm ___ I said that. I apologize.

8 🔊 PRONUNCIATION

Say each word. When does the sound of the underlined letter or letters change?

1 afr<u>ai</u>d   alc<u>o</u>hol   <u>a</u>pologize   <u>a</u>sk
2 <u>a</u>gain   <u>a</u>way   <u>a</u>lcohol   <u>a</u>ppointment
3 ca<u>ll</u>   norma<u>l</u>   practica<u>l</u>   technica<u>l</u>
4 wa<u>l</u>k   s<u>a</u>le   ta<u>l</u>k   s<u>aw</u>
5 h<u>our</u>   <u>your</u>   <u>our</u>   fl<u>our</u>
6 b<u>ear</u>   n<u>ear</u>   b<u>ear</u>   p<u>ier</u>
7 bea<u>ch</u>   ea<u>ch</u>   a<u>ch</u>e   chea<u>p</u>

9 Grammar revision

THE PAST   THE PRESENT

A 'Unreal' or 'imaginery' situation in the present. ➡

⬅ B Very recently in the past with some clear effect on the present ➡

⬅ C At some time between the past and the present that is not mentioned. ➡

A **Look at the three 'situations' above. Then read aloud the following sentences. Which 'situation' above, A, B or C, does each sentence go with?**

1 If I were Ed Bondy, I wouldn't go to the old pier.
2 He's been drinking. That's why he can't think clearly.
3 He's been drunk before. Many times.
4 I've been to Venice Beach myself. Several times.
5 I'd buy a house there if I had more money.
6 Many famous people have lived there.
7 I've been working very hard, so I can't concentrate very well on this exercise.

B **What are the missing words in each sentence?**

1 If I ___ you, I wouldn't go out without a coat.
   A were   B would be   C am

2 It ___ raining recently. That's why the street is so wet.
   A is   B was   C has been

3 I've never ___ such terrible weather before.
   A been seeing   B seen   C saw

4 It's the worst weather we ___.
   A 've ever had   B 've been having   C 're having

5 Just think, if you were on Venice Beach at this moment, the sun ___.
   A was shining   B would shine   C would be shining

6 Do you think you ___ happier if you were there now?
   A will be   B are   C would be

10 🔊 Listening

A **You are going to hear a conversation between a woman (W) and a man. The woman and the first man (1st) are talking about a second man (2nd), who is not there. Listen. Then tick (✓) the correct answers to the questions.**

1 Who is going to come soon?
   W [ ]   1st [ ]   2nd [ ]

2 Who argued with the woman a few minutes ago?
   W [ ]   1st [ ]   2nd [ ]

3 Who gives someone something?
   W [ ]   1st [ ]   2nd [ ]

4 Who doesn't count something because it's too dark to do it?
   W [ ]   1st [ ]   2nd [ ]

5 Who doesn't want to answer a personal question?
   W [ ]   1st [ ]   2nd [ ]

6 Who seems to have a transport problem?
   W [ ]   1st [ ]   2nd [ ]

7 Who is not going to argue about the problem?
   W [ ]   1st [ ]   2nd [ ]

8 Something bad is probably going to happen to someone. Who is that person?
   W [ ]   1st [ ]   2nd [ ]

B 👤👤 **Now answer these questions.**

1 What kind of job or work do you think the first man does?
2 Who do you think the second man is?
3 What is going to happen?

19 THE STORM

1 🗣 TALK ABOUT THE PICTURES

1 Tell your partner who you think the woman is.
2 What do you know about her?
3 How does the weather change from the first
   picture to the third picture?

2 🔊 READING

DAY 7 : SUNDAY : EVENING : VENICE BEACH

'What am I doing here? I wish I were back at the
hotel,' Bondy thought. He was walking along the dark
and deserted beach. It was very windy. A few drops of
rain fell. He wondered if a storm was coming.

Ten minutes later he was still walking. The wind
was stronger. Suddenly there was a flash of lightning
and he saw the dark shape of a pier just in front of
him. There was someone standing on it.

'Is that you, Andrea?' he shouted.

'Of course it is. Come here,' she shouted back.

He came closer, but he didn't like being there at all.

'Why did you ask me to come here, for God's sake?'

'Don't you remember shouting at me the last time
we had an argument? I didn't want that to happen
again where people could hear you,' she told him.

There was another flash of lightning.

'Let's go to the end of the pier. There's a roof over
that part of it,' Andrea said.

He followed her, but then he suddenly stopped
walking. Somehow he knew that he was making a
mistake. They were almost at the end of the pier.

'How did you get here?' he asked.

'By car, of course. I rented one at the airport.'

At first he didn't realize what was wrong, but when
he did, he began to feel afraid.

'But you can't drive,' he whispered.

3 COMPREHENSION CHECK

A Find the words in the text that mean these things.

1 What you can say about the weather when one moment your hat is on your head and the next moment it isn't.
2 Something you can say about a place when you don't see any people there.
3 What you do when you want to know something and ask yourself a question about it.
4 Very strong wind and usually heavy rain.
5 A sudden bright light in the sky just before a storm.
6 What you see when you see only the form of something or someone.

B 👤👤 Discuss these questions with a partner. Begin with the question or questions that you find easiest to answer.

1 Why do you think the beach was deserted?
2 How did the weather change from the time Bondy left the hotel to the time he saw the pier?
3 Why do you think Ed used the words 'for God's sake' in one of the questions he asked Andrea?
4 What was the reason Andrea gave for asking him to come to the pier?
5 What do you think was her real reason for asking him to come there?
6 What was wrong with Andrea's answer to the last question Ed asked her?

4 TALK ABOUT IT

👤👤 First connect the two parts of each sentence below. Then ask your partners the questions.

1 Why do some people feel afraid
2 What are you
3 What would you think if you
4 What kind of weather do you
5 Describe the

A suddenly saw a flash of lightning?
B when they see lightning?
C like?
D kind of weather you hate.
E afraid of?

5 FORM & MEANING

A 👤👤 Which pairs of sentences mean more or less the same thing? When is there an important difference in meaning?

▼ GRAMMAR 24D, p. 124

1 A I wouldn't like to be out in this weather.
  B I don't like being out in this weather.

2 A I like to walk in the rain.
  B I enjoy walking in the rain.

▼ GRAMMAR 25B, p. 125

3 A Let's stop talking about the weather.
  B Let's not talk about the weather any more.

B 👤👤 Now repeat the sentence or sentences that you might say in the following situations.

A You are looking out of the window and the weather is very bad outside.
B You are unhappy because you are out in very bad weather.
C You want to say that sometimes you walk in the rain and like it.
D You don't want to spend any more time talking about the weather.

C Choose the correct words to complete each question. Sometimes two choices are possible.

1 What do you like ___ when the weather is fine?
  A to do B doing C do

2 Do you enjoy ___ on a beach when it is sunny?
  A to lie B lying C when you lie

3 What would you do if you were walking in a park and it suddenly began ___?
  A raining B to rain C rain

4 Do you hate ___ inside when it is sunny outside?
  A to be B being C be

5 Would you like to go on talking about the weather or should we stop ___ about it now?
  A talking B to talk C that we talk

6 Yes, let's ___ about something else.
  A talk B talking C to talk

👤👤 Now ask your partners the complete questions.

6 QUICK REVISION ('TO DO'/'DOING')

A Complete each sentence with the infinitive (to . . .) or the gerund (–ing) form of the word in brackets ( ).

EXAMPLES

(*do*)　　What do you want <u>to do</u> this evening?

(*argue*)　Did Ed remember <u>arguing</u> with Andrea before?

▼ GRAMMAR 24A–D, p. 124; 25A–B, p. 125

1　(*do*)　　Do you enjoy ___ exercises like this?
2　(*do*)　　What would you like ___ this evening?
3　(*watch*)　When was the last time you spent the evening ___ television?
4　(*listen*)　Do you enjoy ___ to classical music?
5　(*listen*)　Would you like ___ some classical music now?
6　(*read*)　Do you remember ___ a conversation between Andrea and a man in Unit 18?
7　(*listen*)　Do you also remember ___ to a conversation between Andrea and another man in Unit 18?
8　(*do*)　　What are the things you can remember ___ when you were a child?

B 👥 **Now ask your partners the complete questions in Exercise A.**

7 🔊 PRONUNCIATION

One word in each sentence below is often written as a weak form ('s, 're, 'd, 've) and is almost always pronounced in its weak form in a full sentence. Underline that word, then read the sentences aloud, using the weak form.

EXAMPLE　It <u>is</u> Sunday evening.　　It's Sunday. . .

1　Ten minutes ago Bondy was in the hotel, but he is outside now.
2　It is windy and the beach is deserted.
3　Ed did not like being there.
4　He wondered why he had come to the pier.
5　Andrea says 'Let us go to the end of the pier.'
6　They are walking towards the end of the pier.
7　Suddenly Ed realizes he has made a big mistake.

8 VOCABULARY PRACTICE

Which word or phrase does not belong with the other three words or phrases?

1　storm　lightning　thunder　sunshine
2　beach　water　go shopping　go swimming
3　enjoy　relax　have a good time　have a bad time
4　get angry　smile　begin to shout　have an argument
5　storm　rain　stay inside　go for a walk
6　on the beach　have a good time　cold and windy　warm and sunny
7　free time　weekend　work　go shopping
8　during the week　have a holiday　work hard　earn money
9　enjoy　happy　smile　afraid

9 REVISION ('HAVE', 'GO', 'MAKE', 'DO')

A Complete each sentence with a form of 'have', 'go', 'make' or 'do'.

EXAMPLE　What do you most hate <u>doing</u> on Monday morning?

1　What do you enjoy ___ in your free time?
2　Do you often ___ to parties?
3　When was the last time you ___ a party in your own home?
4　Do you ___ any special exercises to keep fit?
5　Do you ever ___ swimming?
6　Did you ___ a good time last weekend?
7　What is your idea of '___ a good time'?
8　How many mistakes have you ___ so far?
9　Are you afraid of ___ mistakes?
10　Would you like to ___ this exercise again?

B 👥 **Now ask your partners the complete questions in Exercise A.**

What do you enjoy doing in your free time?

I enjoy going to the cinema.

10 TALK ABOUT IT

A 👥 **First, study the six questions below. Then choose at least two of the situations and discuss them with a partner.**

1 Suppose you were alone in a deserted place, and you suddenly saw a dark shape coming towards you. What would you do?

2 How do you usually feel when you're on a beach and what do you usually do when you're there?

3 How do you usually feel when you're back at work on Monday morning?

4 What would you do if you were at a party and you didn't know anybody there?

5 What would you do if you were on a beach, having a good time and suddenly it began to rain very heavily and got very windy?

6 What would you do if you were staying in a good hotel and some people in the next room were having a terrible argument and making a lot of noise?

B **Here are some possible answers. Which situation in Exercise A do you think each answer goes with? Can you find any answers that are possible for more than one situation?**

A Pick up the telephone and complain about it.

B I wouldn't stay there very long.

C It all depends on the weather.

D I really don't know because I've never been in such a situation.

E That would depend on a lot of things, but in normal circumstances I'd probably introduce myself to at least one person and try to begin a conversation.

F Sometimes I wish I weren't there. Sometimes I'm glad to be there. It all depends on what kind of weekend I had and what I have to do during the coming week.

G It's hard to say. Perhaps I'd run away.

C 👥 **Now look again at the questions in Exercise A. Answer at least one more question you couldn't answer before.**

11 🔊 LISTENING

A **Before you listen, answer these questions about the picture.**

1 Who are the two people?
2 What are they doing?
3 How do you think the man feels?
4 What do you think might happen next?

B **Now listen to the first conversation. Then complete the sentences below.**

1 Ed doesn't believe Andrea because he knows she can't ___.
2 He becomes very angry because he is sure she is ___ to him.
3 He is also sure that they are not ___ on the pier. Andrea ___ brought someone with her.
4 'Stop it! You're ___ me!' she says.

C **Now listen to the second conversation. Then answer these questions.**

1 Who is the man that Andrea is talking to?
2 Where are they?
3 What happened to Ed Bondy?
4 What does Andrea think the man should have done?
5 Why didn't the man do it?
6 Why isn't the man worried about it?
7 What do you think Andrea is going to do in a few minutes?
8 What is the advice the man gives her?

83

20 AFTER THE STORM

1 👥 TALK ABOUT THE PICTURES

1 What time of day do you think it is?
2 Where do you think the man slept last night?
3 What is the man pointing at?
4 What do you think happened on the pier last night?

2 🔊 READING

DAY 8 : MONDAY : DAWN : THE OLD PIER

Every morning, just after dawn, a police car drives along the beach at Venice, California. There are always two police officers in it. The morning after the storm, they saw an old man standing in the water near the old pier. The car stopped and officer Macnab got out. She walked on to the pier. Then she leaned out and looked down. She could see a very old sleeping bag in a narrow space on the shore at the base of the pier. She knew that tramps sometimes slept there when it rained.

'Did you sleep down there again last night, Danny?' the police officer shouted.

The old man was washing his face. 'Yep,' he said.

'It's not safe to do that, Danny, especially when the tide is high. I've told you that before. What would have happened if a big wave had come and washed you into the sea?'

The old man nodded. 'Yep, you're right. It was dangerous out here last night, but not for me. I was tryin' to get some sleep when it happened.'

'When what happened, Danny?'

The old man looked up at the sky. The sun was rising slowly. 'I heard a man and a woman talking. Then another man came. I think you'll find him out there somewhere,' he said.

'Who? Out where, Danny?'

The old man pointed to the water beyond the pier. Just then a wave washed a dark shape a little closer to the shore. It was a man's body.

👥 **Which sentences below are true? Which are false? Read something aloud from the text that gives you the answer each time.**

1 Police officer Macnab had never seen the man standing under the pier before.
2 She probably thought that Danny was very dangerous.
3 When Danny saw the police officer, he probably was afraid and wanted to run away.
4 The place that Danny slept in last night is not a very good place to spend the night.
5 When Danny said 'You'll find him out there,' the police officer had already seen the dead body.

3 COMPREHENSION CHECK

Which explanations do you agree with? Correct the explanations you disagree with.

1   If you sleep in a *narrow* space, you have very little space around you.
2   When you stand on a *shore*, you can usually see water close to you.
3   A *tramp* usually has a job and usually sleeps in a nice bed in a nice house.
4   When the *tide* comes in, the water along the shore is far away from you and when the tide goes out, the water is very near to you.
5   If you are in a very *dangerous* place or situation, something good will probably happen to you.
6   If you see someone's *body* in the water, perhaps that person is swimming – or perhaps he or she is dead.

4 TALK ABOUT IT

🯅🯅 **With a partner, discuss the question or questions you find easiest to answer.**

■   What do you think Danny probably does during the day?

■   Describe two different places he perhaps slept in last week.

■   Describe the clothes Danny probably wears.

■   Describe the food Danny probably eats.

■   What are some of the differences between your life and Danny's life?

■   What do you think Danny heard and saw during the storm?

5 FORM & MEANING

A 🯅🯅 What's the difference?

▼ GRAMMAR 26A–B, p. 125
1   What happened when a big wave came and washed Danny into the sea?
2   What would happen if a big wave came and washed Danny into the sea?
3   What would have happened if a big wave had come and washed Danny into the sea?

B 🯅🯅 Here are some possible answers to the questions in Exercise A. Which answer goes with which question?

A   He'd probably drown.
B   Thank God that didn't happen last night. He'd probably be dead now.
C   What? But that didn't happen.

C Match the two parts of each question.

1   What happened when you
2   What would happen if you
3   What would have happened if you

A   had won a million dollars last year?
B   won a million dollars last year?
C   won a million dollars this year or next year?

🯅🯅 **Ask your partners the complete questions.**

D Say the best way to complete each sentence.

1   If I won a lot of money, I ____ it all very quickly.
     A spent   B had spent   C would spend

2   If I had won $1,000,000 last year, I ____ it all by now.
     A spent   B had spent   C would have spent

3   If I were a tramp like Danny, my life ____ very different now.
     A was   B were   C would be

4   If Ed Bondy ____ to the old pier last night, he would still be alive now.
     A hadn't gone   B hasn't gone   C didn't go

5   If I had gone out in that terrible storm last night, I ____ very wet.
     A would have got   B got   C would get

6 QUICK GRAMMAR REVISION

A Each question has a word missing. Fill in the blanks.

▼ GRAMMAR 26A–B, p. 125

1   How would your life be different if you ___ a tramp like Danny?
2   If you won a lot of money, what is the first thing you ___ buy?
3   What would be different about Ed Bondy's life now if he ___ never left the hotel last night?
4   What do you think Ed would ___ done if he had known what Andrea planned to do?
5   What kind of house ___ you buy if you had millions and millions of dollars?
6   How would you have felt yesterday morning if you ___ spent the night sleeping under a pier?
7   ___ you have gone out yesterday evening if there had been a terrible storm?
8   If you could change one thing about your life now, what ___ it be?
9   What would you do now if you ___ police officer Macnab?
10 What do you think the tramp, Danny, would ___ done if officer Macnab hadn't arrived?

B 👥 How many questions in Exercise A can you answer? Discuss them with your partners.

> If I were a tramp like Danny, I wouldn't have . . .

7 🔊 PRONUNCIATION

A Say the words aloud. When does the sound of the underlined letter or letters change?

1   fl<u>oo</u>r   f<u>ou</u>r   w<u>o</u>rd   st<u>o</u>rm
2   sh<u>o</u>re   w<u>o</u>rd   w<u>o</u>rk   w<u>o</u>rld
3   f<u>oo</u>t   f<u>oo</u>d   p<u>u</u>t   g<u>oo</u>d
4   b<u>o</u>dy   h<u>o</u>t   kn<u>ow</u>ledge   kn<u>ow</u>
5   sh<u>ou</u>lder   sh<u>ou</u>ld   c<u>ou</u>ld   w<u>oo</u>d
6   <u>ea</u>ch   f<u>ea</u>r   n<u>ea</u>r   p<u>ie</u>r
7   spl<u>a</u>sh   c<u>a</u>sh   w<u>a</u>sh   fl<u>a</u>sh

B Now listen and check your answers.

8 QUICK VOCABULARY REVISION

A 👥 What are the words for the parts of the body (1–12)?

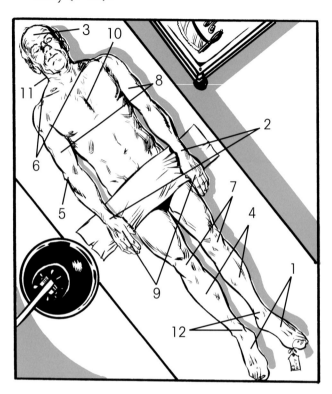

B Now match the words in the box with numbers 1–12.

head	feet	knees	elbow	chest	hands
neck	ankles	shoulders	arms	wrists	legs

C Which word doesn't belong with the other three?

1   head   face   thumb   nose
2   hands   feet   thumb   fingers
3   feet   toes   ankles   wrists
4   hands   feet   walk   stand
5   mouth   finger   point   hands
6   swim   body   sand   water
7   hands   hold   carry   knees
8   feet   arms   hands   carry
9   ears   listen   hear   speak
10 gaze   stare   eyes   lips
11 elbow   leg   knee   foot
12 neck   head   body   voice

9 FIND THE MISSING SENTENCES

A **Police officer Macnab is asking the tramp (Danny) questions. Choose a sentence from Exercise B opposite to fill each gap (0–9). Gap 0 has already been filled as an example.**

B **The missing sentences.**

A That's a man's name, not a woman's name.
B I never eat in restaurants.
C It was too dark.
D Thanks for your help.
E A man and a woman.
F She had an accent.
G Why do you say that?
H And what happened then?
I I remember now.
J I think it was the woman's name.

MACNAB How many people did you see?
DANNY I didn't see them. **0** _C_ . I only heard their voices.
MACNAB How many voices were there?
DANNY First I heard two people talking. **1** ___ .
MACNAB What did they say?
DANNY I'm not sure. I couldn't hear them very well. But I think they were having an argument.
MACNAB **2** ___ .
DANNY Because they sounded angry. I heard the man say 'I'll take you to . . .' Let me think '. . . Mario's'.
MACNAB Mario's? Do you mean that new restaurant on Ocean Boulevard?
DANNY I don't know. **3** ___ .
MACNAB Is that all you heard?
DANNY No. Then he said 'If you don't like it, you can walk.' Something like that.
MACNAB **4** ___ .
DANNY Nothing. They stopped arguing. But about ten minutes later, I heard another man's voice. He shouted 'Is that you?' Then he said a name. **5** ___ It sounded like 'Andy' or something like that.
MACNAB **6** ___ .
DANNY I know, but that's what it sounded like. No, wait a moment. **7** ___ . It was 'Andrea'. That was the name. Yeah.
MACNAB Is there anything else you can remember?
DANNY Yeah. There was something funny about the woman's voice. She didn't sound American. **8** ___ . I think she was English, or something like that.
MACNAB All right, Danny. **9** ___ .

10 🔊 LISTENING

A **First, listen to the complete conversation in Exercise 9A.**

👤👤 **Now read aloud the conversation with a partner. One of you is MACNAB. The other is DANNY.**

B **Now listen to another conversation. Then answer these questions**

1 Who do you think the first woman is?
2 Which city is she phoning from?
3 Why is she phoning?
4 Where did someone take Andrea after the murder?
5 What happened then?
6 What is the other important information that Macnab has?
7 Do you think this is very important information for the woman who phoned?
8 What do you think the woman who phoned is going to do after she gets this information?

21 A NAME AND A MOTIVE

1 CONVERSATION

A 🔊 **Listen to the first part of the conversation.**

DAY 8 : MONDAY : LATE MORNING : SFPD

FERRANTE   Who killed Bondy? Any ideas?

KOVALSKI   I think the question should be 'Who had him killed?'

FERRANTE   Oh, so, you think a professional hitman did it?

KOVALSKI   Yes, I do. Probably the same hitman that killed Hellman.

FERRANTE   Who do you think paid the hitman?

KOVALSKI   I'm not sure. But I have a name and a motive.

FERRANTE   Go on. I'm listening.

KOVALSKI   The name is Andrea Dare. She lives in Portland. She's the head of a company that makes computer software.

FERRANTE   And the motive?

KOVALSKI   Perhaps Bondy was selling her information about one of the products his company was developing.

FERRANTE   But why would she have him killed?

KOVALSKI   He knew too much about her. He was dangerous – far more dangerous than Hellman had been.

FERRANTE   Can you prove any of this?

KOVALSKI   Not yet. That's why I want to go to Portland.

FERRANTE   Go to Portland? Why?

KOVALSKI   To talk to Ms Dare, face to face.

FERRANTE   How will that help you to prove anything?

KOVALSKI   It won't – but if I see her, perhaps I'll know whether she's lying to me or not.

FERRANTE   I can't let you go to Portland, Ros. It's out of the question.

B 🔊 **Now listen to the complete conversation, which includes a second part.**

2 COMPREHENSION CHECK

A Which explanations do you agree with? Correct the explanations you don't agree with.

1 A *professional* is someone who doesn't do anything for money.
2 A *hitman* is someone who hits a ball or something else.
3 When you *prove* something, you show that it is true.
4 When people say 'It's out of the question', they usually mean they will talk some more about it and try to decide if it is possible.
5 You can *miss* a plane, a bus or a train but you can't *catch* a plane, a bus or a train.
6 If you *waste* time or money, you spend it on the wrong things.

B Complete the questions below.

1 ___ Kovalski think Andrea killed Bondy?
2 Is it possible that she had ___ killed?
3 What could ___ been her motive?
4 ___ does Kovalski want to go to Portland?
5 Why does she think she can ___ a better job than the Portland police?
6 Why does Ferrante think that she ___ stop talking?
7 What do you think Kovalski is ___ to do as soon as possible?

C 👥 **Now discuss the questions in Exercise B. Don't try to answer questions 5, 6 and 7 until you have listened to both parts of the conversation at least once.**

3 FORM & MEANING

A 👥 **Which pairs of sentences mean more or less the same thing? When is there an important difference in meaning?**

▼ GRAMMAR 28A–B, p. 126

1 A Who killed Bondy?
  B Who did Bondy kill?

2 A Why did Andrea kill him?
  B Why did Andrea have him killed?

3 A Who paid someone to kill him?
  B Who had him killed?

B 👥 **Here are some answers to the questions in Exercise A. Which questions? Which answer is the answer to two of the questions?**

A Andrea Dare.
B Probably a professional hitman.
C She was afraid he would tell people what he knew about her.
D But she didn't. She paid someone to do it.
E As far as I know, he didn't kill anybody.

C Match the two parts of each question.

1 Do you ever
2 How often do
3 How much does it usually cost
4 When was the last time you
5 Do you have other things

A to have it cut?
B had it cut?
C cut your own hair?
D you have it cut?
E done for you?

D 👥 **Now ask your partner the complete questions in Exercise C.**

Do you ever cut your own hair?

No, I don't.

4 Grammar revision

A Make each pair of sentences into a single question.

EXAMPLE   Someone killed Bondy. Who?
QUESTION   Who killed Bondy?

▼ GRAMMAR 28A–B, p. 126

1 Someone wants to go to Portland. Who?
2 Kovalski wants to talk to someone. Who?
3 Someone wants to ask Andrea some questions. Who?
4 Something happened to Bondy. What?
5 Someone had him killed. Who?
6 Andrea had someone killed. Who?
7 Someone spent the night under the pier. Who?
8 Danny (the tramp) heard someone talking. Who?
9 Something happened after Danny heard them. What?

B Each sentence below is longer than necessary. There is a much shorter and better way to say these things using 'have', 'has' or 'had'. What is that 'shorter and better' way?

EXAMPLE   Why did Andrea pay someone to kill Bondy?
ANSWER   Why did Andrea have Bondy killed?

1 Why don't you pay someone to cut your hair?
2 Where can I go and pay someone to clean a leather jacket?
3 How much does it cost when you pay someone to repair your shoes?
4 You should pay someone to repair this telephone.
5 Andrea always pays someone to make her clothes.
6 Larry Knowles paid someone to build a house in Napa Valley.

5 Vocabulary

👤👤 **Read sentences 1 to 9 aloud. Your partner has to read aloud a sentence from A to I that has the opposite or almost the opposite meaning.**

EXAMPLE

I'm not sure.   There's no doubt about it.

1 I'm not sure.
2 It's out of the question.
3 I caught the train.
4 It's very safe.
5 There's a storm coming.
6 Go on. I'm listening.
7 I did it myself.
8 I've forgotten all about it.
9 I've got evidence.

A Can't we talk about something else?
B I remember it very clearly.
C This wonderful weather is going to last.
D There's no doubt about it.
E I had it done.
F Let's talk about it.
G I missed it.
H I can't prove it.
I It's terribly dangerous.

6 Talk about it

👤👤 **Choose at least two questions below. Talk about each question for more than one minute but no longer than three minutes.**

1 Which of the things below would be out of the question for you? Explain why.
   ■ Changing your job or the place where you now live.
   ■ Walking to work or school tomorrow.
   ■ Flying to New York and staying in the best hotel there the weekend after next.
   ■ Going skiing near your home tomorrow.

2 What do you sometimes have done for you? Why don't you do it yourself?

3 Think of something you *usually* do yourself but which you would like to have done for you? What is it? Why don't you have it done?

7 FIND THE MISSING SENTENCES

A 👥 **First, discuss these questions with a partner.**

1 What do you think Kovalski has just done?
2 Look at the man she is shaking hands with. Who could he be?
3 What do you think she is going to do next?

B Some sentences are missing from the conversation below. Choose a sentence from Exercise C to fill each gap (0–9). Gap 0 has already been filled as an example.

MAN   Are you Rosalind Kovalski?
KOVALSKI **0** _D_ .
MAN   My name is Sam Fernandez, Portland Police Department. **1** ___.
KOVALSKI Thank you. I want to talk to Ms Andrea Dare, who lives here in Portland. She's probably at work now. **2** ___.
MAN   Yeah. I know where it is. **3** ___.
KOVALSKI Yes, please. **4** ___.
MAN   No. **5** ___. Is she expecting you?
KOVALSKI **6** ___.
MAN   How do you know she'll be in her office now?
KOVALSKI Well, she's the head of the company. **7** ___.
MAN   A surprise visit, in other words.
KOVALSKI Exactly. And it's important it should be a surprise.
MAN   **8** ___.
KOVALSKI I hope you won't be offended if I don't answer that question now. **9** ___. I'll explain later.

C The missing sentences.

A I'm here to help you in any way I can.
B It'll take about an hour to get there.
C I'm assuming she at least keeps normal office hours.
D Yes, I am.
E Is it very far?
F No, she isn't.
G There's a good reason.
H Do you mind if I ask why?
I Here's the address of her office.
J Do you want me to take you there now?

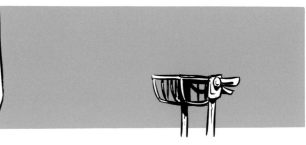

8 🔊 LISTENING

A First listen to the complete conversation between Kovalski and Fernandez. Then check your answers to Exercise 7B.

B Now listen to another conversation. Then complete the sentences below.

1 The first person wants to know if Kovalski has an ___.
2 He also wants to know what she wants to talk to Andrea Dare ___.
3 Kovalski says it's a very ___ matter.
4 Afterwards, Kovalski speaks to Andrea Dare's personal ___.
5 This person tells Kovalski that Ms Dare is in a very important ___ and doesn't want to be ___.
6 Kovalski says that she has some very important ___ that Ms Dare will be very ___ in.
7 She says it will ___ everybody a lot of ___ if Ms Dare sees her now.
8 She also says that if she leaves now, without ___ Ms Dare, the Portland Police will have to come and ___ her later.
9 This could ___ serious ___ for Ms Dare and her ___.

22 NEWS TRAVELS QUICKLY

1 👤👥 TALK ABOUT THE PICTURES

What do you think Sergeant Kovalski is going to ask Andrea? Think of at least four questions.

2 CONVERSATION

A 🔊 Listen to the first part of the conversation.

DAY 8 : MONDAY : AFTERNOON : ANDREA'S OFFICE

KOVALSKI	Thank you for seeing us, Ms Dare. I know you're busy.
ANDREA	Yes, I am, very busy. So be as brief as possible.
KOVALSKI	I'll try. Have you ever heard of a company called GCS?
ANDREA	Of course I have. Why?
KOVALSKI	Do you know anything about RAINBOW 3?
ANDREA	Of course I do. It's similar to a product we're developing.
KOVALSKI	Similar? How similar?
ANDREA	Very similar.
KOVALSKI	Very similar? Isn't that unusual?
ANDREA	No. The two products are competing for the same market. Why shouldn't they be very similar? People expect them to do more or less the same things. It's only natural, isn't it?
KOVALSKI	I'm sorry, Ms Dare. I know very little about computer software.
ANDREA	Yes. That's obvious, isn't it? Why are you asking me these questions?

KOVALSKI	Well, you see . . . I'm investigating the death of Tom Hellman. He was an employee of GCS. He committed suicide.
ANDREA	Yes. I know what happened.
KOVALSKI	Pardon? Did you say you know what happened?
ANDREA	Yes, that's exactly what I said.
KOVALSKI	You seem to know a lot about GCS.
ANDREA	I don't know much about them at all. But news like that travels very quickly in this business.
KOVALSKI	I'm sorry. Perhaps I'm wasting your time.
ANDREA	Then please don't waste any more of it. I asked you to be as brief as possible.
KOVALSKI	Do you mind if I ask you one more question?
ANDREA	It depends on the question!

B 🔊 Now listen to the complete conversation, which includes a second part.

3 COMPREHENSION CHECK

A Find the words or phrases in the conversation that mean these things.

1 A short way of saying 'Say only what is necessary, and don't waste time.'
2 What happens when two or more people or organizations try to sell the same thing to the same people.
3 A place or situation in which people buy and sell things.
4 A way of saying 'This is very normal. It's what you should expect to happen.'
5 A word which means 'very easy to see or understand'.
6 What the police or other people do when they try to find out why something happened.
7 Someone who works for someone else.

B Correct the explanations you don't agree with.

1 If you *expect* something to happen, you don't believe it will happen before it happens.
2 If something is *obvious*, it isn't clear what it means.
3 When Andrea says 'It depends on the question,' she means 'Yes, I'll answer any question you want to ask me.'
4 If someone asks you 'Do you mind if I ask you a question?' and you say 'Yes, I do,' it means 'All right. Ask the question.'
5 If you *hardly know someone*, you have perhaps met that person once or twice but that is all.
6 When Andrea says to Kovalski 'You seem to have problems with your hearing?' she is worried about Kovalski's health.

C 👤👤 Complete the questions. Then discuss answers to them with your partners.

1 Why does Andrea want Kovalski ___ ___ as brief as possible?
2 Why does she think it's 'only natural' that the two products are very ___?
3 Is it true that Andrea hardly ___ Ed Bondy?
4 Why did Kovalski ask the LA police not to tell anybody about the murder ___ she had spoken to Andrea?
5 How did Andrea ___ that Ed Bondy was dead?

4 FORM & MEANING

A 👤👤 Explain the difference in meaning.

1 A Have you heard any news about Ed Bondy?
   B Have you heard the news about Ed Bondy?

▼ GRAMMAR 29A–B, p. 127

2 A Andrea asked Kovalski to be as brief as possible.
   B Andrea told Kovalski to be as brief as possible.

3 A You know a lot about that company.
   B You seem to know a lot about that company.

4 A English is easy to learn.
   B English seems easy to learn.

B Repeat the sentences above that fits each situation.

A You have already heard some news about Ed Bondy. You don't know if the person you're speaking to has heard it, too.
B Andrea said 'Be as brief as possible' and not 'Could you please be as brief as possible?'
C I don't know. But I have the feeling that you know a lot about that company.
D It is a fact that English is easy to learn, and not an opinion, feeling or general impression.

5 TALK ABOUT IT

👤👤 Choose at least one question and discuss it with a partner.

■ What are some things about yourself that you hope are obvious to people when they see you for the first time?

■ What are some things that you think often waste your time?

■ Why do you think Kovalski wanted to see Andrea, and not just talk to her on the phone?

■ Do you think Ed Bondy told his secretary that he was going to Venice Beach?

6 GRAMMAR ('ASK' OR 'TELL')

A Complete the second sentence in each pair using the words 'asked' or 'told'.

EXAMPLES
'Take the medicine twice a day,' the doctor said.
The doctor *told me to take* the medicine twice a day.

'Please phone me every day,' my mother said.
My mother *asked me to phone* her every day.

1 'Please phone me every day, too,' my brother said.
My brother ___ ___ ___ ___ him every day, too.

2 'You must be very careful with your money,' my father said.
My father ___ ___ ___ ___ very careful with my money.

3 'Please send us a postcard,' my parents said.
My parents ___ ___ ___ ___ them a postcard.

4 'And please write a letter to us every week,' they said.
They also ___ ___ ___ ___ a letter to them every week.

5 'You must fasten your seat-belt,' the flight attendant said.
The flight attendant ___ ___ ___ ___ my seat-belt.

6 'Would you show me your credit card?' the man in the hotel said.
The man in the hotel ___ ___ ___ ___ him my credit card.

7 'Please pay the cashier at the front desk,' the waiter in the restaurant said.
The waiter in the restaurant ___ ___ ___ ___ the cashier at the front desk.

8 'Wait for the green light before crossing the street,' a policeman shouted.
A policeman ___ ___ ___ ___ for the green light before crossing the street.

B Think of at least three things people have asked or told you to do recently. The sentences below may help you.

- A few days ago someone asked me to . . .

- A month ago a policeman told me to . . .

- Last week, a teacher asked/told me to . . .

7 TYPICAL RESPONSES

A First complete each of the sentences below.

1 Do you ___ if I ask you a few questions?
2 I hope I'm not ___ your time.
3 Do you know anything ___ a company called 'Daring Solutions'?
4 Have you ___ met the head of the company, Andrea Dare?
5 She ___ two men killed. Didn't you know?
6 Are you interested ___ hearing more about her?
7 ___ you like me to phone you this evening and tell you the rest of the story?
8 Goodbye. It's been nice ___ to you.

B Now match each of the questions in Exercise A with a 'typical response'.

A Yes, I do, but not very much. Why?
B Yes, I am, but I'm afraid I have to leave now. I have an appointment.
C No, I don't. Go ahead.
D Thanks. Take care.
E That's very kind of you, but I'd prefer to read about it in the newspaper.
F No, you're not. Don't worry about that.
G No, I haven't – but I've heard her name before. Why?
H No, I didn't. Who were they? And what was her motive?

C 👥 **Now work with a partner. One of you reads the completed questions (1–8) one at a time, from Exercise A. The other (with the book closed) has to respond to the question. You can use the responses from Exercise B or other responses you think are fairly 'typical'.**

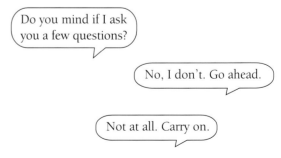

Do you mind if I ask you a few questions?

No, I don't. Go ahead.

Not at all. Carry on.

8))) Listening

Robert Keller and Silvina Arcante are talking to Larry Knowles in his office. Listen. Then choose the best answer to each question.

1 Who has made a 'serious accusation'?

    A Probably Robert or Silvina.
    B Larry Knowles.
    C Ed Bondy.
    D Someone else who is not mentioned.

2 What is the 'serious accusation'?

    A Someone has stolen money.
    B Information has been sold.
    C The wrong information has been given.
    D Someone has come to work late.

3 When do you think this conversation began?

    A Just after they hear the news about Ed Bondy.
    B The weekend when Ed was murdered.
    C A week or so after Ed was murdered.
    D The morning or afternoon after Ed was murdered.

4 What do you think Ed Bondy's secretary tells Larry Knowles?

    A She thinks Ed is in hospital after an accident.
    B She tried to phone Ed at home but there was no answer.
    C The police have just given her some bad news.
    D She thinks Ed is away on business.

5 What do you think Larry finds out at the end of the conversation?

    A Something about Andrea Dare.
    B Something about a trip to Venice in Italy.
    C The news that Ed is dead.
    D Something about Steve Ferrante.

9 How to sound more interested

A))) First, listen to the two conversations.

Conversation 1
A Ed Bondy is dead.
B Oh.
A Yes. He was murdered.
B Oh. I didn't know that.
A And Andrea Dare has been arrested.
B Oh. Why?
A Isn't it obvious? The police think she was connected with the murders.
B Oh.

Conversation 2
A Ed Bondy is dead.
B Is he? What happened?
A He was murdered.
B Was he, really? Who did it?
A I'm not sure. But Andrea Dare has been arrested.
B Has she? You don't think she killed him, do you?
A I don't know, but she's probably connected with the murders, isn't she?

B 👥 Discuss these questions with a partner.

1 In which conversation does Speaker B seem to be more interested?
2 Underline the words that Speaker B uses to show more interest.

C Now complete the conversation below with 'Is', 'Did', 'Was' or 'Were'.

A Andrea is in prison now.
B **1** ___ she? Why?
A She was connected with Bondy's murder.
B **2** ___ she? How? In what way?
A She paid someone to kill him.
B **3** ___ she? Why did she do that?
A Bondy knew too much about her.
B **4** ___ he? What, for example?
A I don't know exactly, but I know this. She and Bondy were lovers.
B **5** ___ they? Are you sure?

D))) Now listen to the conversation and check your answers.

EPILOGUE

1 👥 TALK ABOUT THE PICTURE

1 What do you think is happening in the picture?
2 Match the words below with the numbers 1–4:

- the prosecutor
- the judge
- the jury
- the defendant

3 What do you think a prosecutor, a judge and a jury do?
4 What are some of the things people say or do in this place?
5 What can happen to a defendant?

2 🔊 READING

NINE MONTHS LATER

DARE ADMITS SHE WAS THERE ON FATAL EVENING

ON THE SECOND DAY of her trial Andrea Dare admitted lying to the police when she told them she had not been anywhere near Venice Beach the night Edward Bondy was murdered there.

'I phoned him at the hotel where he was staying. He didn't want me to come there. He sounded very worried, but didn't want to talk about it on the phone. He asked me to meet him at the old pier. When I got there, I couldn't see him anywhere. I waited for half an hour but I felt afraid, and the weather was very bad, too, so I left,' she said.

Under questioning by chief prosecutor Ken Ishihara she also admitted she and Bondy had been lovers.

'He didn't want anyone to know about our relationship. He thought it would look bad. He was afraid people would think he was selling information to me. And he was afraid he would lose his job.'

Dare denied that she had anything to do with Bondy's murder.

'I loved him very deeply,' she claimed, and then broke down in tears.

'My client is innocent, and we will prove it,' her lawyer, Alfred Lobato said.

The trial is expected to continue for at least a week.

👥 **Discuss with your partner how Andrea explains the following things.**

1 Why – according to Andrea – did she go to the old pier and not to Bondy's hotel?
2 What – according to her – happened when she got to the old pier?
3 Why did she decide to leave?
4 Why – according to Andrea – didn't Bondy want other people to know about his relationship with Andrea?

3 COMPREHENSION CHECK

Find the words in the reading text that mean the following things.

1 To say you made a mistake or did something that was bad or which perhaps seems bad.
2 To say you did something that perhaps was very good but which other people perhaps believe you did not do.
3 To say you did not do something which other people say that you did do.
4 What you have with someone who is your friend – or perhaps your lover.
5 The opposite of 'guilty'.

4 🔊 LISTENING

A Andrea is being questioned by her lawyer, Alfred Lobato. Listen. Then choose the best answer, A, B or C.

1 Andrea says she lied to the police because:
  A it would seem bad if she told the truth.
  B she felt guilty but didn't want to admit it.
  C she knew her phone call had something to do with Bondy's death.

2 When – according to Andrea – did Ed realize he was being followed?
  A When she phoned him at the hotel.
  B Before she phoned him.
  C After she phoned him.

3 Who does she say is really guilty?
  A She is, because she phoned him at the hotel.
  B The people who were following Ed.
  C Ed, because he went to the old pier.

B 👤👤 How many different lies do you think Andrea tells here? Repeat each one.

5 FORM & MEANING

A 👤👤 Which sentences mean more or less the same? When is there an important difference in meaning? If there is a difference, can you explain what that difference is?

1 A Does it seem bad to lie?
  B Is it bad to lie?

2 A Did Ed look afraid that night?
  B Did Ed sound afraid that night?

3 A Do you feel younger than you look?
  B Are you younger than you look?

▼ GRAMMAR 30, p. 127

4 A Would it be better if Ed hadn't gone to the old pier that night?
  B Would it have been better if he hadn't gone to the old pier that night?

5 A What would be different about you if you had been born in San Francisco?
  B What would have been different if you had been born in San Francisco?

B 👤👤 Here are six possible answers? But which questions are they answers to?

A Yes, sometimes I do, and sometimes I don't.
B Yes, he did. I saw him so I know.
C Yes, he would probably be alive now.
D Yes, he probably wouldn't have been killed.
E I'd probably speak much better English.
F I would have grown up speaking English.

C Complete the sentences below with the following words.

feel	would feel	seem
would have felt	sound	look

1 Listen to this. How does it ___?
2 How do I ___ in these new clothes?
3 I think I ___ better now if I had gone to bed earlier last night.
4 I think I ___ better yesterday if I had had a good night's sleep.
5 I always ___ better if I get a good night's sleep.
6 Some things in English ___ more difficult than they really are.

6 WHAT ARE THE MISSING WORDS?

A Ken Ishihara, the prosecutor, is questioning Andrea. Some words (1–10) are missing. Can you guess what they are?

ISHIHARA You say that you went to the old pier and waited for Mr Bondy.

ANDREA Yes. Exactly.

ISHIHARA And when he didn't come, you left.

ANDREA Yes, I **1** ___ back to my hotel.

ISHIHARA Were you worried about Mr Bondy? Were you worried about the man you **2** ___ you loved?

ANDREA Yes, of course I **3** ___. I wondered what had happened to him.

ISHIHARA Really? But you didn't phone the hotel afterwards, did you?

ANDREA No, I **4** ___.

ISHIHARA Why not? Why didn't you try to find out **5** ___ had happened to him?

ANDREA Because . . . because . . .

ISHIHARA Yes? Go on.

ANDREA It's very difficult to explain.

ISHIHARA **6** ___ it? Isn't it true that you already knew what had happened to him?

ANDREA No, it **7** ___.

ISHIHARA You knew he was dead, didn't you? You were there when he was killed, **8** ___ you?

ANDREA No. No, I wasn't.

ISHIHARA You paid the man who killed Mr Bondy. You **9** ___ him killed, didn't you?

ANDREA No, I didn't. Someone followed Ed to the pier and killed him before I got there. I had nothing to do with it.

ISHIHARA You don't really expect us to believe that, do you?

ANDREA Yes, I **10** ___. I'm innocent.

B Here are five of the ten missing words. Where do they go?

weren't	say	do	didn't	was

7 GRAMMAR

A Which of the questions, A or B, do you think a prosecutor like Ken Ishihara will probably use when trying to prove that someone is guilty or is lying?

▼ GRAMMAR 31, p. 128

1 A Are you guilty?
  B You're guilty, aren't you?

2 A You had your lover killed, didn't you?
  B Did you have your lover killed?

3 A Are you telling the truth?
  B You aren't telling the truth, are you?

4 A You don't expect us to believe you, do you?
  B Do you expect us to believe you?

B Match the beginning of each question (1–6) with the last part of that question (A–F).

1 It's a nice day,
2 It isn't a very nice day,
3 You speak English,
4 You understood the last exercise,
5 You didn't find it too difficult,
6 You don't think this is too difficult,

A didn't you?
B don't you?
C do you?
D isn't it?
E did you?
F is it?

THE VERDICT

8 👥 TALK ABOUT THE PICTURE

1 Where do you think Kovalski and Ferrante are?
2 They are waiting for some very important information. What could it be?
3 How do you think they both feel at the moment?
4 Are you also waiting for some very important information at the moment? If so, what is it that you want to know?

9 📻 LISTENING

A **Before you listen, match the words and phrases below (1–9) with the explanations (A–I).**

1 It's been tough for you, hasn't it?
2 The jury's still out.
3 reach a verdict
4 any minute now
5 cover a case
6 I'm going to miss you
7 cops
8 prevent
9 industrial espionage

A decide if someone is guilty or innocent
B slang for 'police'
C what a reporter does who reports what is happening in court
D very very soon
E I know you've had a lot of hard work to do and some difficult problems recently.
F I'm sorry you're leaving and that I won't see you
G getting and selling confidential information that a company doesn't want other companies or organizations to know about
H the people who have to reach a verdict still can't decide what the verdict is
I stop something before it happens

B **Now listen to the conversation. Are the following sentences true or false?**

1 When the conversation begins, Kovalski and Ferrante have just heard the verdict.
2 Kovalski has been working only on one case.
3 It seems that Ferrante is not going to be Kovalski's boss for much longer.
4 Ferrante wants to go to Florida or Southern California and play golf when he retires.
5 The first phone call Kovalski gets is from a reporter in Los Angeles.
6 Ferrante is going to work for companies that want to sell confidential information.
7 The second phone call is from the same person who made the first one.
8 This person gives Kovalski some information she never expected.
9 Kovalski decides after the second phone call definitely to work for Ferrante in his new business.

C 👥 Now discuss these questions.

1 What do you think the verdict was?
2 Which verdict are they talking about?
3 How do you think Ferrante and Kovalski feel about it?
4 What do you think Kovalski may do in the future?

TAPESCRIPTS

1 SERIOUS PROBLEMS

PAGE 8. EXERCISE 2. READING   (See page 8)

PAGE 11. EXERCISE 9. LISTENING

MIGUEL	Excuse me, but . . . uh . . .
KOVALSKI	Yes?
MIGUEL	Haven't we met somewhere before?
KOVALSKI	No, I don't think so.
MIGUEL	I'm sure we have, you know.
KOVALSKI	Really? I'm sorry but I don't remember you. And I never forget a face.
MIGUEL	Oh, well, anyway, my name's Miguel. Miguel Hernandez.
KOVALSKI	My name's Kovalski. Ros Kovalski.
MIGUEL	Pleased to meet you, Ros.
KOVALSKI	Same here.
MIGUEL	Are you enjoying the party?
KOVALSKI	No, not really.
MIGUEL	No? Why not? I mean, what's wrong?
KOVALSKI	Nothing is wrong. Nothing at all. I just don't like parties very much. I never go to them.
MIGUEL	But you're at one now.
KOVALSKI	I know.
MIGUEL	Well, why did you come to it if . . . if you don't like parties very much?
KOVALSKI	It's a little difficult to explain. Let's just say I'm here because of my job. Is that why you're here?
MIGUEL	No. I'm not here because of my job. I came because I wanted to. I'm really enjoying it.
KOVALSKI	What do you do, Miguel?
MIGUEL	I work for GCS. Have you ever heard of us?
KOVALSKI	I think so. Doesn't GCS stand for Global Computer Systems?
MIGUEL	Yes, that's right. We're out in Foster City. What about you?
KOVALSKI	What about me?
MIGUEL	Yes. What do you do?
KOVALSKI	I work for the SFPD.
MIGUEL	SFPD?
KOVALSKI	Yes. SFPD.
MIGUEL	What does SFPD mean? I mean, what do the initials stand for?
KOVALSKI	Well, the 'SF' stands for 'San Francisco'.
MIGUEL	And what does 'PD' stand for? Wait a minute. I think I know. Are you a . . . ?
KOVALSKI	I'm a detective. Yes. I work for the San Francisco Police Department.

2 HOTLINE

PAGE 12. EXERCISE 2. CONVERSATION

Part one. (See page 12)

Part two.

MAN	More powerful? Do you mean it does a lot of things RAINBOW 2 didn't do?
WOMAN	Yes, sir. That's exactly what I mean. How many people on your staff are using the new version?
MAN	About twelve people. But they all say the same thing. They were happier with the old program. Perhaps it didn't do as many things as RAINBOW 3 does. But it was much easier to use – much easier to work with.
WOMAN	Perhaps your staff needs more training with the new version. We can arrange that for you.
MAN	Hmm . . . yes, perhaps you're right, but . . . well . . .
WOMAN	Just a moment, sir. I'll put you in touch with Linda Shawcross. She's the manager of the Hotline team. She'll be glad to discuss your problems and suggest some solutions.

3 JOB INTERVIEW

PAGE 16. EXERCISE 2. READING   (See page 16)

PAGE 19. EXERCISE 10. LISTENING

TOM	Just listen to me, please.
ED	Do you know what the time is?
TOM	I'm sorry it's late. I really am.
ED	Late! It's midnight. No, it's after midnight. And it's Sunday too! Or rather, it was Sunday.
TOM	Did I wake you?
ED	Yes, you did. I was asleep.
TOM	I'm sorry. But I need . . . I need to talk to you.
ED	Where are you calling from?
TOM	I'm at home.
ED	Can anybody hear you?
TOM	No. I'm alone.
ED	What about your wife?
TOM	She isn't here. She's in Boston. Didn't you know that? Didn't I tell you that?
ED	Tell me what?
TOM	That my wife has left me. She doesn't live with me any more.
ED	Is that why you're phoning now? To tell me about your personal problems with your wife?
TOM	No, that isn't why I'm phoning.
ED	Then why are you telling me all this about your wife?
TOM	But you asked me about her.
ED	I asked you where you're calling from. I just want to be sure that nobody can hear you.

TOM	No. I'm alone. I told you.
ED	Well, what is it, for God's sake? Why are you calling me, then?
TOM	It's about this thing. You know what I mean. It isn't right.
ED	What do you mean it isn't right? What isn't right?
TOM	What we're doing with RAINBOW. It isn't right.
ED	What *we're* doing? You mean, what *you're* doing with RAINBOW. It's your problem, not my problem.
TOM	What do you mean? How can you say that?
ED	I'm not the Project Manager. You are.
TOM	What do you mean? You're in it, too.
ED	No. You took the money. I didn't.
TOM	Yes, but . . .
ED	There are no 'buts' about it. Not for me. You took the money. Now do what you have to do.
TOM	I just can't. I can't go on.
ED	Oh yes, you can. So do it! Or you really will have a problem!
TOM	But I tell you it isn't right.
ED	I can't listen to this any more. I haven't time for this . . . stupid conversation. You took the money. You're the Project Manager. You know what to do. Now do it!

4 A CHANGE OF PLAN

PAGE 20. EXERCISE 2. CONVERSATION

Part one. (See page 20)

Part two.

ROBERT	I'm leaving for the airport in a few minutes. I'll read it on the way.
LARRY	You're going to London. Right?
ROBERT	Yes. I'm staying there for four nights – until Sunday morning.
LARRY	I'd like you to change those arrangements. I want you to be back here by Saturday evening.
ROBERT	Saturday evening? Why?
LARRY	We're having a special crisis meeting Sunday morning, and I want you to be here for it. By the way, some people in England are already working with RAINBOW 3. I'd like you to talk to them while you're there.

PAGE 23. EXERCISE 9. LISTENING

A

ROBERT	Oh, hmm. I travel a lot, so that's a difficult question. But I think . . . let me see . . . yes, I think it was a journey I took two years ago, when I flew to Japan, then to Australia, and then to Europe before coming back to San Francisco.

B

ROBERT	Ahh, that's much easier to answer. By boat, but just around the Bay here. I mean a real boat. A boat with sails. I love sailing. I have a small boat here in San Francisco . . . well, actually it's across the bay, at Sausalito . . . and at the weekends I go sailing whenever it's possible.

C

ROBERT	It can depend on the traffic. But usually about thirty-five minutes. Sometimes a little longer . . . . I often leave home very early in the morning, before the rush hour . . . around six or six-thirty . . . and there isn't much traffic then.

D

ROBERT	I drive there. It's the only possible way. There are no buses or trains that go there.

E

ROBERT	Yes, I do. Very frequently. And I don't enjoy flying at all. Even though I travel Business Class, and sometimes First Class. But it's part of my job. I do it because I have to, not because I want to.

5 A DARK TUNNEL

PAGE 24. EXERCISE 2. READING   (See page 24)

PAGE 27. EXERCISE 9. LISTENING

Extract 1

ROBERT	Hello, Margaret? This is Robert.
	(*pause*)
	At the airport. San Francisco Airport. Listen, I've just been told there's going to be a delay.
	(*pause*)
	I'd like you to fax Sue O'Brian in London.
	(*pause*)
	Just tell her that the plane may be late.
	(*pause*)
	Yes, Sue O'Brian in our London office. She's going to be at the airport in London to meet me. I don't want her to wait longer than necessary.
	(*pause*)
	Yes. Give her my flight number so that she can find out from flight information when it arrives.
	(*pause*)
	What? Oh, yes, of course. Just a moment. It's here, I think. No, it must be the other pocket. Just a moment. It's E–I five–six–nine. That's 'E' for Elisabeth and 'I' for India. Have you got that?
	(*pause*)
	Yes, that's all. Thanks for your help, Margaret.
	(*pause*).
	Thanks, Margaret. Oh, by the way . . .

Extract 2

PILOT	Good evening. My name is John Williams and I'm your pilot this evening. I'd like to apologize for the delay. We had a slight technical problem which we've solved now. We'll be on our way in a few minutes. I'll be speaking to you again when we're in the air. I'd like to thank you again for flying European International.

Extract 3

PILOT	Good evening again, ladies and gentlemen. This is your pilot with some flight information. Our flight time to

London this evening will be twelve hours and twenty minutes – but since we left San Francisco about an hour ago, that leaves about eleven and a half hours to go. The weather *en route* is good, but we expect a little rain by the time we reach England. The temperature in London is . . . uh . . . normal for this time of the year. Sixty-two degrees Fahrenheit which is . . . uh . . . about sixteen degrees centigrade. We'll be back with some more information during the flight, so . . . uh . . . sit back and we hope you enjoy the flight and . . . uh . . . once again, thank you for flying European International.

6 IS THIS A GRAMMAR LESSON?

PAGE 28. EXERCISE 2. CONVERSATION

Part one. (See page 28)

Part two.

KOVALSKI	If he wrote it on his computer, why weren't his fingerprints on the computer keyboard?
FERRANTE	What? No fingerprints on the keyboard?
KOVALSKI	No. The keyboard was wiped clean.
FERRANTE	What do you mean? Who wiped it clean?
KOVALSKI	I don't know.
FERRANTE	Jesus, Ros.
KOVALSKI	But that isn't all.
FERRANTE	That isn't all what?
KOVALSKI	That isn't all I don't like about this case. It isn't the only reason I don't think it was suicide.
FERRANTE	Yeah? What's the other reason?
KOVALSKI	The money in his pocket. When he died, he had more than four hundred dollars in his pocket.
FERRANTE	So what? What's so strange about that?
KOVALSKI	He got the money from the bank that morning. Monday morning. At nine o'clock. Doesn't that seem a little strange to you?
FERRANTE	No. Lots of people still use cash. Lots of people still go to the bank and take out money.
KOVALSKI	Not when they're planning to commit suicide in a few hours' time. People who are planning to kill themselves don't usually go to the bank at nine, take out a lot of money and then jump out of a window less than two hours later.

PAGE 31. EXERCISE 9. LISTENING

INTERVIEWER	Our guest this morning on Metro Radio here in San Francisco is Sergeant Rosalind Kovalski, a member of the San Francisco Police Department. How long have you been a detective, Sergeant Kovalski?
KOVALSKI	For five years.
INTERVIEWER	Why did you become a police officer?
KOVALSKI	Perhaps because of my father. He was a police officer in New York. He was killed when I was twelve.
INTERVIEWER	What happened to him?
KOVALSKI	He tried to stop a bank robbery. He was alone and there were four bank robbers. One of them shot him.

INTERVIEWER	But why did you want to do the same job? Do you think your father would be happy if he knew?
KOVALSKI	No, I don't think so.
INTERVIEWER	Why not?
KOVALSKI	Well, once, not long before he was killed, I was . . . oh . . . ten, perhaps eleven years old . . . and I told him that when I grew up, I wanted to do the same job he did.
INTERVIEWER	And what'd he say?
KOVALSKI	He didn't say anything. But I don't think he thought it was a good idea.
INTERVIEWER	Why? Did he think that only a man could do his job?
KOVALSKI	No, I think he thought I couldn't do the job. He didn't think I was . . . hard enough. Tough enough.
INTERVIEWER	So, in a way, perhaps you do this job because . . . because you wanted to show him that you could do it. Is that what you're saying?
KOVALSKI	Not exactly. I thought I could do it. And so I wanted to find out who was right. And when I found out that I was right . . . that I could do it, well, by then I also knew that it was what I wanted to do.
INTERVIEWER	So, you like your job?
KOVALSKI	Yes, of course. That's why I do it. I wouldn't want to do any other job. I know I can do it, and I like what I do. And that's why I do it. Because I like it.

7 HOW WAS YOUR FLIGHT?

PAGE 32. EXERCISE 2. CONVERSATION

Part one. (See page 32)

Part two.

ROBERT	Serious problems? Can you give me some idea what kind of problems you're talking about?
SUE	I think they're all problems with RAINBOW 3. I understand that several customers have been complaining about it.
ROBERT	Complaining? You mean, they aren't satisfied with it?
SUE	No, I'm afraid they aren't.
ROBERT	Why not?
SUE	That's what Linda wants to talk to you about.
ROBERT	You said there were several problems. Did you really mean only a few? Or are there more than that?
SUE	I . . . uh . . . it's really difficult for me to answer that question. I don't deal with the customers directly. Linda does. That's why I think it's better if she tells you.

PAGE 35. EXERCISE 9. LISTENING

MAN	So you want to reserve a single room for five nights. How would you like to pay?
WOMAN	By credit card. But before I do that, can I just check on a few details. Where is Venice exactly?
MAN	About half an hour away from the airport by car.
WOMAN	And how close are you to the ocean?
MAN	You walk out of the front door, turn left, and there it is.

WOMAN   Uh-huh. And what about restaurants and things like that?

MAN   There must be at least fifty close to the hotel.

WOMAN   How close?

MAN   Between five and fifteen minutes on foot. Even closer by car.

WOMAN   I see. Now, one of the reasons I'm coming to Los Angeles is to visit the Getty Art Museum. Is that within walking distance, too?

MAN   Uh . . . well . . . not really, but you can get there by bus. We can arrange that, as well as all the other usual tours.

WOMAN   Hmm. All right. Could you reserve a room for me, please?

MAN   All right. Can I have the number and the expiry date of your credit card, please?

WOMAN   Yes. Just a moment, please . . . I can't find my credit card. Tell you what. I'll fax the number to you in a few minutes with a written confirmation.

MAN   All right. Remember to include the expiry date, please.

WOMAN   Yes. I'll do that. Goodbye. Oh, no, wait. One last thing. Is it true that Charlie Chaplin used to live there?

MAN   No, he didn't live here. But he had rooms here, and he used to spend the weekends here during the summer. At least, so I've been told.

WOMAN   Oh, I see. How interesting. All right. I'll fax you my credit card number with my confirmation in a few minutes.

MAN   Thank you. Don't forget the expiry date, please.

8   CUSTOMER COMPLAINTS

PAGE 36. EXERCISE 2. CONVERSATION

Part one.   (See page 36)

Part two.

ROBERT   What's the answer to that question?

LINDA   I don't know. I was hoping you could tell me.

ROBERT   But Linda, I'm not the Technical Director – Ed Bondy is. He was Tom Hellman's boss. If anybody can answer that question now, it's Ed, not me.

LINDA   I . . . well . . . perhaps I shouldn't say this but . . .

ROBERT   Yes? Go on. I'm listening.

LINDA   Ed is a very good engineer. Everybody says that. But he isn't very easy to talk to.

ROBERT   Isn't he?

LINDA   No, he isn't. Perhaps that's why you're here and he isn't.

ROBERT   I'm afraid I don't know Ed very well.

LINDA   I don't think anyone knows him very well.

PAGE 39. EXERCISE 9. LISTENING

ROBERT   What about you? How well do you know Ed?

LINDA   I've met him a few times. That's all.

ROBERT   Has he been here? To London?

LINDA   No. I've met him in Foster City once or twice. By the way, talking about Foster City, do you remember Silvina Arcante?

ROBERT   Of course I remember her. I liked her very much. She

was very good at her job. Do you know what she's doing now?

LINDA   Yes. I suppose you know that she's back in Argentina.

ROBERT   Yes. I heard that. She went back last year, after she quit her job at GCS. She's in Buenos Aires, isn't she?

LINDA   Yes, where she was born. And she's started her own business there.

ROBERT   What kind of business?

LINDA   She gives advice to companies and businesses about the . . . uh . . . you know . . . the best use of computer software and hardware.

ROBERT   Hmm. That's interesting. She's very familiar with RAINBOW, isn't she?

LINDA   Of course. She was on the team that began developing the new version.

ROBERT   But then she left the company.

LINDA   Yes. Then she left the company.

ROBERT   You and she were good friends, weren't you?

LINDA   Yes, we still are. I phone her once or twice a week.

ROBERT   Really? Hmm . . . uh . . .

LINDA   Yes?

ROBERT   Do you have her business number in Buenos Aires?

LINDA   Yes. Why?

ROBERT   I'd like to talk to her. Do you have the number with you?

LINDA   No, but I can give it to you tomorrow. But she isn't in Buenos Aires right now.

ROBERT   No. Where is she?

LINDA   San Francisco.

ROBERT   San Francisco? Really? Why?

LINDA   There's a conference there. You can phone her secretary tomorrow. She'll tell you where Silvina is staying.

ROBERT   Yes. Perhaps I can see her when I go back.

9   AN UNEXPECTED VISITOR

PAGE 40. EXERCISE 2. READING   (See page 40)

PAGE 43. EXERCISE 10. LISTENING

Conversation 1   (Exercise 10A)

WONG   Margaret? This is Peter Wong in Finance. I need to talk to Ed Bondy this afternoon.

WOMAN   I'm sorry, Peter. Mr Bondy doesn't want to be disturbed this afternoon. He's finishing a report which he wants to present at the special meeting this Sunday.

WONG   But this is very important. I have to talk to him.

WOMAN   The only time I can fit you in is this morning.

WONG   I have two meetings this morning. The only time I'm free is this afternoon.

WOMAN   I'm sorry, Peter. I really am. But that isn't possible. You know what Mr Bondy's like.

He doesn't want to be disturbed by anybody this afternoon, not even the President of the United States.

WONG   Oh, Jesus. Sorry, Margaret. It's not your fault, I know, but . . . Uh . . . all right, I'll cancel one of my meetings this morning. When can you fit me in?

WOMAN   Ten-thirty.

WONG   An hour from now?

WOMAN   Yes. Can you be here at ten-thirty?

WONG   Yes, I can. I'll have to, won't I?

WOMAN   And I'm afraid I can give you only fifteen minutes. He's seeing someone else at ten forty-five.

WONG   All right. Thanks, Margaret.

Conversation 2 (Exercise 10B)

WOMAN   Mr Bondy's office.

KOVALSKI   Who am I speaking to?

WOMAN   This is Mr Bondy's secretary. Who's calling?

KOVALSKI   Is Mr Bondy going to be in his office this afternoon?

WOMAN   Mr Bondy can't see anybody this afternoon. Who is this, please?

KOVALSKI   Do you mean he can't see anybody or he doesn't want to?

WOMAN   Did you want to make an appointment?

KOVALSKI   No, I'll call again this afternoon.

WOMAN   I've just told you that he can't see anybody this afternoon.

KOVALSKI   So, he's going to be in his office but he doesn't want to see anybody. Is that right?

WOMAN   Who is this? . . . Who is this? Hello? Hello?

10   SECURITY ARRANGEMENTS

PAGE 44. EXERCISE 2. CONVERSATION

Part one. (See page 44)

Part two.

KOVALSKI   . . . When I was in Hellman's office the other day, I noticed that there was no security camera there.

TUCKER   No, we don't have cameras in every office, but like I said, there's always a camera outside, in the corridor.

KOVALSKI   But I didn't see a camera in the corridor outside his office, either.

TUCKER   No, you see, he was supposed to move from that office to a bigger one on the seventeenth floor this week. But, of course, he didn't because . . . well, you know what happened.

KOVALSKI   The other people in his office had already moved. Is that right?

TUCKER   Yep. He was the last person up there, all on his own. That's why all the other desks and equipment had been moved out – and why there was no camera in the corridor.

KOVALSKI   Thanks again, Mr Tucker. I'd like to take another look at Hellman's office now, if you don't mind.

TUCKER   Of course not, Sergeant. Do you want me to come up with you?

KOVALSKI   No, that won't be necessary. But thank you all the same.

PAGE 47. EXERCISE 10. LISTENING

ROBERT   Good evening. My name is Robert Keller. I have a very important message for Silvina Arcante.

SECRETARY   Ms Arcante is not in Buenos Aires at the moment. She's in San Francisco.

ROBERT   Yes, I know she's in San Francisco. I live in San Francisco myself and I have a very important message for her. Can you send it to her?

SECRETARY   I'll give you the number of her hotel, and you can contact her. You live there so it will be very easy for you.

ROBERT   But I'm not in San Francisco at the moment. I'm in London, but I'd like to meet Silvina there Saturday afternoon. Can you tell her that?

SECRETARY   Please. One moment. I . . . I'm writing this down. You are in London and you want to meet Silvina Saturday afternoon. Pardon me, but what was your name again?

ROBERT   Robert Keller. That's K–E–L–L–E–R.

SECRETARY   Where do you want to meet her?

ROBERT   At the hotel. And that's my next question. Can you tell me where she's staying in San Francisco?

SECRETARY   At the Pacific Orient Hotel.

ROBERT   Oh, yes. I know where that is.

SECRETARY   And when do you want to meet her Mr Keller?

ROBERT   At three in the afternoon. In the coffee-shop.

SECRETARY   In the coffee-shop of the hotel?

ROBERT   Yes. Shall I repeat the message?

SECRETARY   Yes, please.

ROBERT   Tell her that Robert Keller phoned from London. I'll be in the coffee-shop of the hotel at three Saturday afternoon and would like to meet her there. It's very, very important. Have you got that?

SECRETARY   Yes. Excuse me, Mr Keller, but London is very far away from San Francisco, isn't it?

ROBERT   Yes, I know it is. Very far. Nine or ten hours by plane. Why?

SECRETARY   Nothing. Can I have the name and telephone number of your hotel. Perhaps Ms Arcante will want to contact you before the meeting.

ROBERT   Yes, of course. Sorry. I should have told you that before. I'm staying at the Barton Hotel.

SECRETARY   Pardon?

ROBERT   The Barton Hotel.

SECRETARY   The . . . uh . . . Button Hotel. And the telephone number?

ROBERT   0171 462 900365.

SECRETARY   You're staying at the Button Hotel, 0171 462 900635

ROBERT   No. The last three digits are 365, not 635.

SECRETARY   Thank you, Mr Keller. I . . . I will give Ms Arcante your message.

ROBERT   Thank you. Sorry if I sounded . . . uh . . . in a bad mood. It's been a long day for me here in London. I'm very tired.

SECRETARY   Yes. I understand, Mr Keller.

11 JUST AFTER MIDNIGHT

PAGE 48. EXERCISE 2. READING   (See page 48)

PAGE 51. EXERCISE 7. LISTENING

ANDREA Hello?
BONDY It's me. I need to talk to you.
ANDREA Jesus! Do you know what time it is?
BONDY It's important. I wouldn't be calling now if it weren't.
ANDREA I hope it is. Important, I mean.
BONDY Listen to me, damn it. A detective came to see me today.
ANDREA Why? What did he want?
BONDY It was a *she*, not a *he*.
ANDREA So? What did this lady detective want?
BONDY She wanted to know about Hellman . . . She asked me how well I knew him. She wanted to know why he phoned me late last Sunday night.
ANDREA She knew? How did she know about that?
BONDY From the records of the telephone company, I suppose. You and I have to meet somewhere. We have to talk about this . . . Are you listening?
ANDREA Stop shouting, Ed. Calm down . . . Perhaps you're right, Ed. Perhaps you're right that we should meet. But it would . . .
BONDY There are no 'buts' about it, Andrea. We have to meet and talk about this. If she finds out what really happened on Monday, you'll be in as much trouble as I am. More, perhaps. After all, this whole damned thing with Hellman was your idea, not mine.
ANDREA Ed! I'm going to tell you one more time and that's all! Listen! Shut up and listen . . . Perhaps we should meet. The question is where.
BONDY Why is that a question? You can come here or I can go there.
ANDREA Jesus, Ed. People say you're a brilliant engineer, so just *think* for a moment. It would be very bad if someone saw us together in San Francisco or here in Portland. Especially now.
BONDY Well, where else can we meet?
ANDREA Do you know where Venice is?
BONDY Venice? You think I'll go all the way to Italy to . . .
ANDREA No, Ed. Venice, California. It's part of Los Angeles. I know a place there. A hotel on the beach. We can meet there Sunday evening.
BONDY Sunday isn't good for me. There's a special crisis meeting here on Sunday.
ANDREA How long is this meeting going to last?
BONDY I don't know, Andrea. How can I?
ANDREA Well, book a seat on one of the evening flights to LA. Get there by seven o'clock. The flight takes about an hour.
BONDY But what if the meeting goes on late into the evening?
ANDREA Find some excuse to get away from it and get to LA no later than seven! I'll be waiting for you at the hotel.
BONDY Just a moment. What's the name of the hotel?
ANDREA The Cadillac Hotel. Cad–ill–ac. Write it down.
BONDY And you're going to reserve the room there?
ANDREA Yes. Uh . . . wait. No. It'll be better if you do that. Don't ask your secretary to reserve the room. Do it yourself . . . and don't use the phone in your office . . . or your home phone. The number is three, one . . . .
BONDY Why can't you do it?
ANDREA Do what?
BONDY Reserve the room.
ANDREA Oh, for God's sake, Ed. Can't you do anything yourself? OK. I'll reserve the room . . . but you make sure you arrive by seven o'clock.

12 I DON'T BELIEVE HIM

PAGE 52. EXERCISE 2. CONVERSATION

Part one.   (See page 52)

Part two.

KOVALSKI . . . I want to know why Bondy didn't tell me the real reason Hellman phoned him.
FERRANTE But if you're right, if Hellman was murdered, and Bondy didn't do it, how did the murderer get into the building? Don't they have any security arrangements there?
KOVALSKI Yes, they do. Good security arrangements.
FERRANTE Well, then, how was it possible for the murderer to get into the building?
KOVALSKI I don't know.
FERRANTE And how was it possible for the murderer to get up to Hellman's office?
KOVALSKI I don't know.
FERRANTE How did he get out of the building?
KOVALSKI I don't know.
FERRANTE Why didn't anybody stop him?
KOVALSKI I don't know.
FERRANTE You keep saying that. Pardon me for saying so, Ros, but there's an awful lot you don't know.
KOVALSKI Let me change my answer, Steve. I don't know *yet*.
FERRANTE You mean, you think you can find out?
KOVALSKI Yes. I think I can find out.
FERRANTE How?
KOVALSKI I have an idea. I'll tell you about it after I look at some videotapes tomorrow.

PAGE 55. EXERCISE 8. LISTENING

TUCKER Hello. Tucker speaking.
KOVALSKI Hello, Mr Tucker. This is Ros Kovalski.
TUCKER Morning Sergeant.
KOVALSKI Good morning, sorry to bother you again, Mr Tucker. It's about the tapes you mentioned.
TUCKER Tapes?
KOVALSKI Yes, videotapes. The visual records of everybody who comes in and leaves the building.
TUCKER Oh, yeah. I'm with you now, Sergeant. What about them?
KOVALSKI I'd like to watch them tomorrow afternoon. Could you arrange that for me?
TUCKER Sure. No problem at all, Sergeant. Do you want me to send them over to you or are you going to watch them here?

KOVALSKI	I'll come there. I may have a few questions to ask about the tapes.
TUCKER	I see, I won't be here tomorrow, so when you come, ask for Andy Hewitt.
KOVALSKI	Sorry? Who should I ask for? Could you spell the last name for me, please?
TUCKER	H-E-W-I-double T. He's a Scotsman. And he's assistant head of security here. If you have any questions, he can answer them.
KOVALSKI	Thank you, Mr Tucker. You've been very helpful.
TUCKER	Just one more thing, Sergeant. What time are you coming here tomorrow afternoon?
KOVALSKI	Uh, well, uh . . . let's see. About five?
TUCKER	Could you make it a bit earlier than that, Sergeant? Andy is on duty here tomorrow between seven-thirty in the morning and four in the afternoon. So if you want to talk to him about anything, you should be here before four.
KOVALSKI	Oh. Hmm. I was going to interview someone tomorrow at four, but . . . uh . . . yes, I think I can change that. All right. Tell Mr Hewitt I'll be there at three-thirty. Is that all right?
TUCKER	Three-thirty? That sounds just fine.
KOVALSKI	Thanks again, Mr Tucker. You've been very helpful.
TUCKER	Always glad to help, Sergeant.

13 CAN I BE FRANK?

PAGE 56. EXERCISE 2. CONVERSATION   (See page 56)

PAGE 59. EXERCISE 8A. LISTENING

ROBERT	And so, that's why I wanted to see you.
SILVINA	Yes, but – why do you want my advice about the project?
ROBERT	Because you're an independent consultant who knows the company well. So you can be more objective than someone inside the company.
SILVINA	But I'm very busy at the moment.
ROBERT	We realize that. That's why I've been authorized to offer you $15,000 a day plus all expenses for the next ten days. Starting immediately.
SILVINA	Hmm. And in return you want me to act as a special consultant again.
ROBERT	Exactly. Well, what about it? Do you accept our offer?
SILVINA	Do you mind if I ask you a few questions before I answer that?
ROBERT	Of course not. Go ahead.
SILVINA	Who would I work with? Who would I give this advice to?
ROBERT	To the Technical Director, of course.
SILVINA	To Ed Bondy?
ROBERT	Yes. Why?
SILVINA	Can I be frank?
ROBERT	Of course.
SILVINA	Ed Bondy is a brilliant engineer. But it would be very difficult for me to work with him again . . . and probably just as difficult for him to work with me.
ROBERT	May I ask why?

SILVINA	Well, . . . uh . . . he and I have had some very serious disagreements.
ROBERT	About what?

PAGE 59. EXERCISE 8B. LISTENING

SILVINA	Well, . . . uh . . . he and I have had some very serious disagreements.
ROBERT	About what?
SILVINA	All sorts of things.
ROBERT	Such as what?
SILVINA	Two things. First of all, Ed said that customers want a version that's far more powerful than the old version.
ROBERT	Do you really disagree with him about that?
SILVINA	Not completely. I think they want a version that does some new things. But not as many new things as Ed thinks are necessary.
ROBERT	Well, then, what exactly do you think the new version should do that the old version doesn't do?
SILVINA	Before I tell you that, let me tell you the second thing we disagreed about.
ROBERT	I'm sorry. Go ahead.
SILVINA	Customers also want the new version to be as user-friendly as the old version. Ed thinks that it doesn't matter if the new version is more difficult to use. He says that power is the only really important thing.
ROBERT	Why?
SILVINA	Perhaps you should ask him that.
ROBERT	I will, but perhaps you could tell me what you think his answer will be.
SILVINA	As you know, the new version will be a lot more expensive than the old version. Ed says that customers will pay the new price only if the new version is far more powerful. I believe they'll pay more only if the new version is more powerful but just as easy to use as the old version was.
ROBERT	Hmm. Silvina. You still haven't answered my question.
SILVINA	Which question?
ROBERT	Do you accept the offer? Will you act as a special consultant for us again if . . . ?
SILVINA	Robert, please listen. I've already explained why that isn't possible and why I want to go back to Argentina as soon as possible. I'm sure you can find another consultant. I'll even help you.
ROBERT	Please let me finish, Silvina. Will you accept the offer if you report to me, and not to Ed Bondy?
SILVINA	Report to you? You mean, I would be working with you and not Ed Bondy?

ROBERT	Exactly.
SILVINA	Hmm. I see. That would make your offer more . . . how shall I say it . . . attractive.
ROBERT	Does that mean you accept it?
SILVINA	Yes. I accept your offer.
ROBERT	Good. In that case, there's no problem.
SILVINA	Hmm. I hope you're right.

14 ARE YOU INTERESTED NOW?

PAGE 60. EXERCISE 1. READING   (See page 60)

PAGE 63. EXERCISE 7B. LISTENING

FERRANTE	I hear you've been watching a video.
KOVALSKI	That's right. I have. I think you should, too.
FERRANTE	Listen, Ros. I have to tell you something. You're spending too much time on this ca . . .
KOVALSKI	Before you say anything more, just watch this. It'll take two or three minutes.
FERRANTE	So, what's so interesting about this?
KOVALSKI	Just watch. You'll be surprised.
FERRANTE	Two men in an elevator. Really fascinating. Ros, I can't let you spend any more . . .
KOVALSKI	This happened a few minutes before Hellman . . . uh . . . let's say 'fell' out of the window of his office on the sixteenth floor. One of these men told the receptionist that they wanted to deliver something to someone on the *fifteenth* floor. As I said, Hellman's office was on the *sixteenth* floor. Now, watch this. There are video cameras on almost every floor of the GCS building. Now this is what video camera 15 D recorded at exactly ten fifty-four and twenty seconds in one of the offices on the fifteenth floor. Look. There were two men in the elevator. But only one of them went to the office.
FERRANTE	What?
KOVALSKI	And remember. Hellman was on the next floor.
FERRANTE	Jeez!
KOVALSKI	Are you interested now?
FERRANTE	Are you saying you think the other guy went up to Hellman's office and pushed him out of the window?
KOVALSKI	Yes. That's exactly what I'm saying.
FERRANTE	But how was that possible?
KOVALSKI	The killer could have used a drug of some kind – probably a spray or a needle – Hellman wouldn't have known what was happening.
FERRANTE	Wait a moment. You said there were cameras on every floor. Have you looked at the videotape from the camera on the *sixteenth* floor?
KOVALSKI	No, I haven't.
FERRANTE	Well, why not?
KOVALSKI	I said there were video cameras on *almost* every floor. There were no cameras on the sixteenth floor – and Hellman was the only person on the sixteenth floor that morning.
FERRANTE	Why? Where were all the other people who work on that floor?
KOVALSKI	They had all moved to new offices on the seventeenth

	floor. Hellman was the last person left on the sixteenth floor, and he was supposed to move to the seventeenth floor, too, the next day. So, Monday was the last day it was possible for anyone to get in and out of Hellman's office without being seen.
FERRANTE	Hmm. But how can you be sure that's what really happened?
KOVALSKI	Before I answer that question, let me tell you something else. I phoned the security company – and they have no record of any deliveries to anybody in the GCS building on that day.
FERRANTE	Jeez. In other words, you think one of those guys was a professional.
KOVALSKI	Yes, someone paid the killer to do it.
FERRANTE	And who do you think that was?
KOVALSKI	It must have been someone inside the company. Someone who knew a lot about Hellman.
FERRANTE	Yeah, but who?
KOVALSKI	I can't be sure – but I think it was probably Ed Bondy.
FERRANTE	Probably? Or possibly?
KOVALSKI	Probably.
FERRANTE	But why? Why would Bondy want to have Hellman killed? What was the motive, Ros?
KOVALSKI	That's what I don't know yet. And that's what I have to find out.

15 CUSTOMERS ALWAYS COMPLAIN

PAGE 64. EXERCISE 2. CONVERSATION   (See page 64)

PAGE 67. EXERCISE 9. LISTENING

LARRY	I think what Ed is saying, Robert, is we usually get a few complaints from a few customers when we bring out a new product.
ROBERT	But these are more than a few complaints – and more than a few customers have made them.
BONDY	Listen! Before we began developing RAINBOW 3, we asked customers all over the world what they wanted. And they all told us the same thing. They want something far more powerful than RAINBOW 2. And that's what we've given them.
ROBERT	But now that they have it, they aren't satisfied with it.
BONDY	I don't have time to argue with you. But before I leave, there's something I want to ask you.
ROBERT	What?
BONDY	I noticed that when you came in this morning, Silvina Arcante was with you. Why?
ROBERT	I've asked her to help me.
BONDY	Help you? What do you mean? How?
LARRY	As you say, Ed, Robert is not an engineer, and I know you don't have enough time to explain certain . . . technical matters to him. That's why I've authorized Robert to employ Silvina as an independent consultant for a week or so.
BONDY	Well, if you want to throw the company's money away, I can't stop you! But just keep her away from me! And now, if you don't mind, I have work to do!

16 JUST A COINCIDENCE?

PAGE 68. EXERCISE 2. READING   (See page 68)

PAGE 71. EXERCISE 9. LISTENING

MAN	Good evening.
BONDY	Good evening. My name is Bondy – B–O–N–D–Y. I have a reservation.
MAN	One moment, sir. Yes, that's right, Mr Bondy. One night. Is that right?
BONDY	Yes.
MAN	Ah yes. Room 509.
BONDY	Is Ms Dare already upstairs in the room?
MAN	Pardon? Who?
BONDY	Ms Dare.
MAN	Is she staying here, sir?
BONDY	Yes, of course. We . . . we're together. But I've just come from San Francisco. She told me she would be here before me.
MAN	Well, I'm afraid nobody by that name has checked in so far.
BONDY	You mean, she isn't here?
MAN	No, sir. I'm afraid not. Uh, did you say you wanted a double room when you made the reservation?
BONDY	I didn't make the reservation. She did.
MAN	Oh, I see. Uh . . . just a moment. Is Ms Dare English?
BONDY	Yes, she is. Why?
MAN	I remember now. I spoke to her when she made the reservation. I thought I noticed an accent. I'm English, myself.
BONDY	Oh?
MAN	Yes. So I remember the lady but . . . unless I'm mistaken, she didn't tell me she would be staying here, as well.
BONDY	She didn't?
MAN	No, sir. But there's no problem. The room reserved for you is a double. Since we thought you would be alone, we're charging you the rate for a single. We'll have to change that, of course.
BONDY	Of course.
MAN	Now, one last thing, sir. Usually when a reservation is made by phone, we get a credit card number. But I didn't, in this case. So . . . uh . . . will you be paying or will Ms . . .
BONDY	Dare. D–A–R–E. I . . . uh . . . I thought . . . that she . . .
MAN	Yes?
BONDY	Nothing. I mean, . . . uh . . . here's my credit card. Will that do?
MAN	Yes, of course. Just a moment, sir.
BONDY	By the way. Is there a bar in the hotel? I'd like a drink while I'm waiting.
MAN	Yes, sir. On the left. Next to the elevator.

17 TWENTY-FOUR HOURS

PAGE 72. EXERCISE 2. CONVERSATION

Part one. (See page 72)

Part two.

KOVALSKI	If Bondy hired the killer, did he do it alone or was someone else involved? And why did he – or they – want Hellman dead? We'll never answer those questions unless you give me another twenty-four hours.

PAGE 75. EXERCISE 9. LISTENING

KOVALSKI	Hellman's murder was planned very carefully.
FERRANTE	Yeah. Of course the murder was planned very carefully.
KOVALSKI	What would have happened if one small thing had gone wrong, Steve?
FERRANTE	Oh, Jesus. Is this another of your trick questions?
KOVALSKI	Just answer it, Steve.
FERRANTE	If one small thing had gone wrong, everything would have gone wrong. There were too many risks.
KOVALSKI	Exactly. That's why I don't think Bondy planned the murder.
FERRANTE	Why not? You say he's a brilliant engineer.
KOVALSKI	He is. But brilliant engineers don't take risks like that.
FERRANTE	Yeah. Perhaps you're right. Let the FBI worry about it now.
KOVALSKI	I think it was a woman.
FERRANTE	What? You think a woman planned the murder?
KOVALSKI	Yes. Only a woman could have persuaded Bondy to take risks like that. Probably a very attractive woman, too.
FERRANTE	You mean Bondy wasn't thinking right.
KOVALSKI	Exactly. And he's worried now. Very worried. So they're probably going to meet somewhere. And if she planned Hellman's murder, she's probably planning something else. Something is going to happen. Something important – and it's going to happen very soon.
FERRANTE	Ros, for God's sakes. I can't give you any more time. You know that.
KOVALSKI	What will happen if I'm right, Steve? If we wait another twenty-four hours, we'll find all the answers we're looking for. If we don't wait, the FBI will find the answers and get all the credit. And what will people say?
FERRANTE	I don't give a damn what people say.
KOVALSKI	People will say that it took the FBI only a few hours to do what we couldn't do in more than a hundred hours of very hard work. And why? Because you didn't wait for another twenty-four hours.
FERRANTE	Goddamn it, Ros. Goddamn it.
KOVALSKI	What does that mean, Steve?
FERRANTE	It means you have another twenty-four hours. That's all.

18 THE OLD PIER

PAGE 76. EXERCISE 2. CONVERSATION (See page 76)

PAGE 79. EXERCISE 10. LISTENING

ANDREA He'll be here soon. In about ten minutes.
MAN Did he argue with you?
ANDREA Yes. He always argues. But he always does what I tell him to do in the end.
MAN Good. Now, the money please.
ANDREA Here it is.
MAN Good.
ANDREA Aren't you going to count it?
MAN I can't. It's too dark.
ANDREA It's all there.
MAN I'm sure it is. It would be very bad for you if it weren't all there.
ANDREA You . . . you have an accent. I mean, you're not an American, are you?
MAN Don't ask questions. It will be better for you if you know as little as possible about me.
ANDREA Yes. You're right, of course. But there's something else.
MAN What?
ANDREA What will happen after you . . . you know . . . do it?
MAN I've already told you. We will leave as quickly as possible. I'll take you back to Mario's.
ANDREA Mario's? Do you mean the restaurant where we met before we came here?
MAN Yes. I'll take you back there. Then you will never see me again and I will never see you again.
ANDREA But, how will I get back to my hotel?
MAN What do you mean? You will go back in your own car, of course.
ANDREA But I came to the restaurant in a taxi.
MAN Why? Why didn't you come by car?
ANDREA I don't know how to drive.
MAN That's your problem, not mine, as they say in this country.
ANDREA But it'll be . . .
MAN If you came by taxi, you can go back in one. When you get to the restaurant, ask them to phone for a taxi for you.
ANDREA But it'll be much easier if you take me back to the hotel in your car.
MAN Easier for you, maybe. Not for me.
ANDREA But it isn't that far. I mean, surely you can . . .
MAN Look, lady. I don't run a taxi service. You know what I do. That's what I do and that's all I do. So if you don't want to take a taxi after I take you back to the restaurant, you can walk!

19 THE STORM

PAGE 80. EXERCISE 2. READING (See page 80)

PAGE 83. EXERCISE 11. LISTENING

First conversation (Exercise 11B)
ANDREA Let's go to the end of the pier.
BONDY Why?
ANDREA There's a roof over that part of it. Come on. You don't want to get wet, do you?
BONDY Why don't you just come back to the hotel with me, now?
ANDREA I have something important to tell you – and I want to tell it to you here, not in the hotel. Now, let's go to the end of the pier . . . What is it now, Ed? Just come with me to the end of the p . . .
BONDY How did you get here?
ANDREA How did I what?
BONDY Get here. How did you get here, damn it?
ANDREA In a . . . by . . .
BONDY Yes? How?
ANDREA By car, of course.
BONDY By car?
ANDREA Yes I rented one . . . at the airport.
BONDY But you can't drive.
ANDREA What? I can't what?
BONDY Drive. You can't drive. Why are you lying to me?
ANDREA Take your hands off me.
BONDY You're lying to me. Who's here with you? Tell me the truth, damn it!
ANDREA Stop it! You're hurting me!

Second conversation (Exercise 11C)
HITMAN Are you all right?
ANDREA What?
HITMAN Are you all right?
ANDREA Yes. I think so. I . . . I didn't know he was so strong. And I never thought you would do . . .
HITMAN What? You never thought I would do what?
ANDREA Do it when he was so . . . so close to me.
HITMAN He had his hands around your neck. If I hadn't shot him then, you'd be dead now.
ANDREA Yes. I realize that. Uh . . . what about the . . . you know . . . the body?
HITMAN What about the body?
ANDREA He was probably carrying identification. Credit card. Something like that. Don't you usually . . . take those things?
HITMAN Yes, usually. But I couldn't this time. You pushed him into the water. What do you expect me to do? Go swimming with the guy?
ANDREA I just think it would have been better if we had taken his credit card and everything so that it would be more difficult to identify him.
HITMAN The way I look at is this. The police would have found out who he is even if I had taken everything from his pockets. Now, we're almost there. Just go into the restaurant. Ask them to call you a taxi.
ANDREA Do I look all right?

HITMAN   Sure. You look just fine. Nobody will ever know that a guy had his hands around your neck a few minutes ago and was trying to kill you. Just relax. Smile. Have a drink until your taxi comes. You know, have a nice evening, as they say here.

20   AFTER THE STORM

PAGE 84. EXERCISE 2. READING   (See page 84)

PAGE 87. EXERCISE 10. LISTENING

First conversation (Exercise 10A)

MACNAB   How many people did you see?

DANNY   I didn't see them. It was too dark. I only heard their voices.

MACNAB   How many voices were there?

DANNY   First I heard two people talking. A man and a woman.

MACNAB   What did they say?

DANNY   I'm not sure. I couldn't hear them very well. But I think they were having an argument.

MACNAB   Why do you say that?

DANNY   Because they sounded angry. I heard the man say 'I'll take you to . . .' Let me think '. . . Mario's'.

MACNAB   Mario's? Do you mean that new restaurant on Ocean Boulevard?

DANNY   I don't know. I never eat in restaurants.

MACNAB   Is that all you heard?

DANNY   No. Then he said 'If you don't like it, you can walk.' Something like that.

MACNAB   And what happened then?

DANNY   Nothing. They stopped arguing. But about ten minutes later, I heard another man's voice. He shouted 'Is that you?' Then he said a name. I think it was the woman's name. It sounded like 'Andy' or something like that.

MACNAB   That's a man's name, not a woman's name.

DANNY   I know, but that's what it sounded like. No, wait a moment. I remember now. It was 'Andrea'. That was the name. Yeah.

MACNAB   Is there anything else you can remember?

DANNY   Yeah. There was something funny about the woman's voice. She didn't sound American. She had an accent. I think she was English, or something like that.

MACNAB   All right, Danny. Thanks for your help.

Second conversation (Exercise 10B)

KOVALSKI   I'm investigating a case here in San Francisco. I think it may be connected with Bondy's murder there in Los Angeles. I'd appreciate any information you could give me.

MACNAB   Well, first of all there was a tramp who was sleeping under the pier where Bondy was killed. He says that Bondy came to the pier last night to meet a woman called Andrea. The tramp says she had an English accent.

KOVALSKI   Andrea? With an English accent? Is that all you can tell me?

MACNAB   No. The tramp says that before Bondy came to the pier, he heard the woman arguing with another man. The man mentioned a place – a restaurant not far from the pier. The other man was probably the killer – a professional – and he took the woman to the restaurant afterwards.

KOVALSKI   The killer took her to a restaurant? Why?

MACNAB   They'd met there before the murder. The woman had come by taxi. I've spoken to the manager of the restaurant. He remembers the woman very clearly. Says he was surprised because she left the restaurant around eight and then came back again an hour later. It was raining very heavily. She asked him to call a taxi for her.

KOVALSKI   Do you know where the taxi took her?

MACNAB   Yes. I called all the taxi companies in the area and one of the drivers remembers taking a woman with an English accent to a hotel near the airport.

KOVALSKI   Do you know the name of the hotel?

MACNAB   Yes, and I checked with the manager. It seems there was a woman with an English accent who stayed there last night. Her name is Andrea Dare. She lives in Portland, Oregon. I can give you her credit card number.

21   A NAME AND A MOTIVE

PAGE 88. EXERCISE 1. CONVERSATION

Part one. (See page 88)

Part two.

FERRANTE   If Dare is in Portland, it's a job for the police in Portland, not for us.

KOVALSKI   Nobody in Portland knows what I know about these two murders. I'm the only person that can ask Dare the right questions.

FERRANTE   How do you know the police in Portland will let you interview her?

KOVALSKI   I've already spoken to them. All I need is your authorization.

FERRANTE   Damn it, Ros.

KOVALSKI   Don't you underst . . .

FERRANTE   Stop talking, Ros.

KOVALSKI   Were you listening to me? Did you understand me?

FERRANTE   Yeah. I was listening very carefully. And I understood every word you said. That's why I think you should stop talking now. You're wasting time.

KOVALSKI   No. You don't understand. Unless I go to Portland, we'll never . . .

FERRANTE   No, this time *you* don't understand, Ros. Unless you stop talking now, you'll miss the plane.

KOVALSKI   Which plane?

FERRANTE   The next plane to Portland. I'll call the police there now and tell them you're coming.

PAGE 91. EXERCISE 8. LISTENING

Conversation one (Exercise 8A)

FERNANDEZ   Are you Rosalind Kovalski?

KOVALSKI   Yes, I am.

FERNANDEZ	My name is Sam Fernandez, Portland Police Department. I'm here to help you in any way I can.
KOVALSKI	Thank you. I want to talk to Ms Andrea Dare, who lives here in Portland. She's probably at work now. Here's the address of her office.
FERNANDEZ	Yeah. I know where it is. Do you want me to take you there now?
KOVALSKI	Yes, please. Is it very far?
FERNANDEZ	No. It'll take about an hour to get there. Is she expecting you?
KOVALSKI	No, she isn't.
FERNANDEZ	How do you know she'll be in her office now?
KOVALSKI	Well, she's the head of the company. I'm assuming she at least keeps normal office hours.
FERNANDEZ	A surprise visit, in other words.
KOVALSKI	Exactly. And it's important it should be a surprise.
FERNANDEZ	Do you mind if I ask why?
KOVALSKI	I hope you won't be offended if I don't answer that question now. There's a good reason. I'll explain later.

Conversation two (Exercise 8B)

GUARD	Good afternoon, may I help you?
KOVALSKI	Yes. My name is Rosalind Kovalski. San Francisco Police Department. This is Detective Fernandez, Portland Police Department. We'd like to speak to Ms Andrea Dare, please.
GUARD	Do you have an appointment with her?
KOVALSKI	No, I'm afraid we don't. However, it won't take long. I have just a few questions I'd like to ask her.
GUARD	Well, could you tell me what it's about?
KOVALSKI	It's very confidential. Could you please tell Ms Dare we're here.
GUARD	Just a moment, I'll have to phone upstairs. Hello? There are two people here from the police who want to talk to Ms Dare . . . You will? Just a moment. Ms Dare's personal assistant would like to talk to you.
KOVALSKI	Good afternoon. My name is Kovalski. I've come from San Francisco specially to see Ms Dare.
PA	I'm afraid Ms Dare is in a very important meeting at the moment and can't be disturbed.
KOVALSKI	What I have to tell her is very important, too. Very important.
PA	I'm very sorry but . . .
KOVALSKI	Look. Please tell Ms Dare that I have some very important information that I think she will be very interested in, and that if she can see me now – for a few minutes – it will save all of us a good deal of time.
PA	I don't think she will be able to see you now.
KOVALSKI	When I say all of us, I mean her company as well as the Portland Police Department.
PA	Are you here on police business? Do you have a . . .
KOVALSKI	If I leave now, without seeing Ms Dare, the Portland Police will have to come and see her later – and that could cause serious problems for Ms Dare and her company. I'm sure she doesn't want that to happen. Aren't you?
PA	Just a moment, please. I'll speak to her.

22 NEWS TRAVELS QUICKLY

PAGE 92. EXERCISE 2. CONVERSATION

Part one. (See page 92)

Part two.

KOVALSKI	What can you tell me about Ed Bondy?
ANDREA	Very little. I hardly knew him.
KOVALSKI	I . . . beg your pardon. What did you say?
ANDREA	I hardly knew him!
KOVALSKI	Pardon? Did you say you hardly knew him?
ANDREA	You seem to have problems with your hearing. Is that why you keep repeating what I say?
KOVALSKI	I don't think so. At least I hope not. You used the past tense. That's very interesting.
ANDREA	What's so interesting about the past tense? I use it all the time.
KOVALSKI	Especially when you talk about people who are dead, like Tom Hellman and Ed Bondy, I suppose.
ANDREA	Yes, exactly. As I said, news travels quickly in the computer software business.
KOVALSKI	Yes, I suppose it does. But not that quickly.
ANDREA	What do you mean?
KOVALSKI	Even Ed Bondy's secretary doesn't know yet that he's dead. I asked the Los Angeles police not to tell anybody until I had spoken to you. So, how did you know Ed Bondy was dead, Ms Dare?

PAGE 95. EXERCISE 8. LISTENING

LARRY	Just a moment. You want me to believe that someone here – someone in, as you say, a very responsible position has sold information about RAINBOW 3 to a competitor? That's a very serious accusation!
SILVINA	I know it is, and I wouldn't have made it if I hadn't thought very seriously about it.
ROBERT	Silvina and I spent most of the weekend talking about it, Larry.
LARRY	Before you go any further, let me find out if Ed Bondy's secretary knows where he is. I think Ed should hear this . . . Hello, Margaret. Do you have any news about Ed, yet? . . . No? . . . I see. Thank you, Margaret.
ROBERT	What's wrong, Larry?
LARRY	Ed Bondy didn't come to work this morning. His secretary tried to phone him at home, but there was no answer.
ROBERT	That's unusual, isn't it?
LARRY	Very unusual! He isn't away on business. As far as we know, he was at home all weekend. So if he isn't there, where is he?
SILVINA	Perhaps he's had an accident.
LARRY	I don't think so. His secretary has already spoken to the police. He isn't in any of the hospitals in this area . . . Hello? . . . Who? . . . Yes, of course I'll speak to him . . . Good afternoon, Lieutenant Ferrante . . . Yes, that's correct. He's our Technical Director . . . No, he didn't come to work this morning . . . What? . . . His body was . . . What? . . . Where? Do you mean Venice, Italy? . . . Oh, I see, in Los Angeles. But why . . . I mean, what was he doing there? . . . No,

I understand. Of course you don't . . . Yes. Thank you . . . I can't believe it.

ROBERT You can't believe what, Larry?

LARRY I just can't believe it. It isn't possible.

EPILOGUE

PAGE 96. EXERCISE 2. READING (See page 96)

PAGE 97. EXERCISE 4. LISTENING

LOBATO Ms Dare, why did you tell the police you did not go to Venice Beach the evening Mr Bondy was murdered?

ANDREA I was afraid they would think I had something to do with the murder if I told the truth. But I'm not guilty. I sometimes feel guilty, but I'm not.

LOBATO One moment. I don't think I understand. You say you aren't guilty but that sometimes you feel guilty. Why do you sometimes feel guilty if you aren't guilty?

ANDREA Because sometimes I think Ed would still be alive if I hadn't phoned him at the hotel.

LOBATO But why do you think your phone call had something to do with Mr Bondy's death?

ANDREA I think someone was following Ed. That's why he sounded so nervous on the phone. He knew he was being followed – and the people who were following him must have been the people who killed him. They must have known he was going to meet me at the old pier. And that's why I sometimes feel guilty. If I hadn't phoned – if I had gone to the hotel without phoning him and met him there, he wouldn't have gone to the old pier. Perhaps that's how they knew where he was going. Perhaps they were listening. And that's why I feel guilty sometimes. Perhaps he would still be alive if I hadn't phoned him at the hotel that night. It would have been better if I hadn't phoned.

THE VERDICT

PAGE 99. EXERCISE 9. LISTENING

FERRANTE You look tired.

KOVALSKI I *am* tired. In fact, I'm exhausted. All the extra work on the Bondy case. And then all the other cases I've been working on.

FERRANTE It's been tough, hasn't it?

KOVALSKI It hasn't been easy.

FERRANTE Any news about the trial?

KOVALSKI The jury's still out.

FERRANTE When do you think they'll reach a verdict?

KOVALSKI Any minute now. A friend of mine – a reporter in Los Angeles – is covering the trial. He's going to phone me as soon as the jury has made their decision.

FERRANTE You know, Kovalski. I'm going to miss you.

KOVALSKI I'm going to miss you, too, Steve. Somehow this place won't be the same without you. What are your plans?

FERRANTE Well, somehow I don't think it's a good idea for me to do what most of the other cops I know do after they retire.

KOVALSKI You mean you're not going to move to Florida or Southern California and spend all your time playing golf.

FERRANTE No, I'm going to start my own business.

KOVALSKI You're not serious, are you? You? A businessman?

FERRANTE Well, the business I plan to go into is . . . (*The phone rings.*)

KOVALSKI Kovalski . . . Oh, hello, Andy . . . They have? When? . . . So, when is the verdict expected? . . . I see . . . yeah, I'll be here, Andy. Thanks.

FERRANTE Was that your friend in L.A.?

KOVALSKI Yeah. The jury has reached a verdict and they're going back into court now.

FERRANTE So, in another few minutes, you'll know.

KOVALSKI Yeah. In another few minutes.

FERRANTE You don't think they'll be stupid enough to believe that story of Dare's, do you?

KOVALSKI I don't know. She doesn't have to prove that's she innocent. The prosecution has to prove she's guilty. You know that as well as I do. I know she's guilty. You know she is. But it isn't easy to prove it.

FERRANTE No, it isn't.

KOVALSKI So, what exactly is this new business of yours?

FERRANTE I'm going to try to prevent industrial espionage.

KOVALSKI Prevent industrial espionage? Wow!

FERRANTE Yeah. A lot of companies are worried about it. So, if a company thinks someone is selling information, it'll be my job to find out who's doing it, and to stop it.

KOVALSKI It sounds very interesting.

FERRANTE If you ever want another job, Ros, I'll have one for you. (*The phone rings again.*)

KOVALSKI Hello? . . . Yes, I'm listening. Go on, Andy . . . What? . . . Oh, God! . . . Shocked? No, I'm not shocked. Surprised and disappointed perhaps, but not shocked . . . Thanks, Andy. I'll buy you a drink the next time you're here. Bye.

FERRANTE Well? What was the verdict?

KOVALSKI Do I have to tell you?

FERRANTE No. I can see it from the way you look.

KOVALSKI Damn it. I was afraid this would happen, but somehow I didn't think it would. Or at least I hoped it wouldn't.

FERRANTE I can't believe it.

KOVALSKI I don't *want* to believe it, but that's what the verdict is.

FERRANTE Jesus, Ros. Jesus! They actually believed her story.

KOVALSKI Perhaps they did. Perhaps they didn't. But the prosecution couldn't prove it. You know . . . I have a strange feeling that someday . . . perhaps soon . . . who knows . . .

FERRANTE Who knows what, Ros? What are you talking about?

KOVALSKI That job you've just offered me. Perhaps I'll take it. And if I do, I have a strange feeling that Andrea Dare and I will meet again.

GRAMMAR SUMMARY

1 REAL TIME IN THE PRESENT

A   NO DEFINITE TIME IN THE PRESENT

1   **Tom *works* for Global Computer Systems. He *comes* from Boston but he *lives* in San Francisco now.**

This is the general present. If it is true now, it was probably true yesterday and will probably be true tomorrow. Sometimes a definite time is mentioned, but it is still *generally* true and not only at that particular, definite time.

2   **I usually *get up* at seven o'clock. But on Sunday I often *get up* a little later.**

Here, 'seven o'clock' seems like a definite time. But the word 'usually' means 'not necessarily *today* at seven o'clock'.

B   UNFINISHED ACTIONS HAPPENING AT A DEFINITE TIME IN THE PRESENT

3   **It is seven o'clock now. People *are getting up* and *going* to work. Some *are* already *working*. A few people *are coming* home.**

Here, 'seven o'clock' means 'a particular or definite seven o'clock – seven o'clock now'. Notice the use of 'be' (am, is, are) with the '–ing' form of the verb.

4   **What *are* you *doing* now? *Are* you *getting up*? *Are* you *going* to work? Or *are* you already *working*?**

These questions are about the real present now – not the *general* or 'no definite time' present. The actions are perhaps going on as you speak, and they are *unfinished* actions.

C   ACTIONS SEEN AS COMPLETE OR FINISHED IN A STORY

5   **Tom *goes* to the window and *opens* it.**

Both the Present Simple (*go/goes*; *open/opens*) and the Present Progressive (am/is/are going, am/is/are opening) are often used in stories. But there is an important difference. When the Present Simple (Example 5) is used, the action is seen as *finished* and *complete*. Compare this with the Present Progressive in Example 6:

6   **Tom *is going* to the window . . . and now he *is opening* it.**

This is like watching someone in slow motion. The action is not seen as complete; it is *unfinished*.

EXERCISE 1 (ANSWERS PAGE 128)

Tick (✓) only the sentences that mean 'This is unfinished now and is probably happening as I speak.'

1   It is almost 11 o'clock and Tom is working.   ☐
2   Tom and I work in the same office.   ☐
3   Jack takes the bus to work.   ☐
4   Jack is taking the bus to work.   ☐
5   The bus is coming.   ☐
6   The bus stops in front of the supermarket.   ☐
7   The bus is stopping in front of the supermarket.   ☐
8   A lot of people are getting on the bus.   ☐

---

2 REAL TIME IN THE PAST

A   ACTIONS THAT HAPPENED AT A DEFINITE TIME IN THE PAST AND WHICH ARE NOW FINISHED

1   **Mr Greenway *used* RAINBOW 2 for three years.**
2   **I know San Francisco well. I *lived* there for five years.**

The use of the Past Simple (*used, lived*) means that these actions happened only in the past. They *do not* continue into the present.

B   THIS HAPPENED AFTER THAT HAPPENED

3   **When Robert *heard* about the delay, he *phoned* me.**

First Robert heard about the delay. Then he phoned me. Both actions are complete. The sentence suggests that Robert phoned me *because* he heard about the delay.

C   UNFINISHED ACTIONS AT SOME DEFINITE TIME IN THE PAST

4   **When the plane took off, the sun *was setting*.**
5   **What *were* you *doing* yesterday at exactly 9.35?**

Use the Past Progressive (*was/were –ing*) to talk about actions that were *unfinished* and perhaps actually going on at a very specific moment in the past. In Example 4, the sky was red and the people on the plane could still see the sun.

6   **At 9.35 yesterday I *was working* in my office. I *was reading* a report.**

This means you began working *before* 9.35. You began reading the report *before* 9.35 and you continued reading it *after* 9.35.

D   ACTIONS OR EVENTS THAT HAPPENED BEFORE OTHER ACTIONS OR EVENTS IN THE PAST

7   **The sun *had set* when the plane took off.**
8   **I *had read* the report when the phone rang.**

The Past Perfect (*had set, had read*) tells us what happened before another action or event in the past. Examples 7 and 8 tell us that the sky was dark when the plane took off, and that I finished reading the report before the phone rang.

EXERCISE 2 (ANSWERS PAGE 128)

Use the correct form of the words in brackets ( ) to complete the sentences.

EXAMPLE
It (*rain*) *was raining* when I woke up yesterday.

1   It (*rain*) ___ for two hours and then stopped.
2   I (*go*) ___ out to lunch at 1 o'clock.
3   It was sunny, but the streets were still wet because it (*rain*) ___ so heavily.
4   When I (*come*) ___ out of the restaurant, the sun (*shine*) ___ .
5   But it (*start*) ___ to rain again when I (*go*) ___ back to the office and I got wet.
6   When I (*finish*) ___ work at 5 o'clock, I (*go*) ___ home.
7   After I (*get*) ___ home, I (*have*) ___ something to eat.

3 BETWEEN PAST AND PRESENT

A ACTIONS THAT STARTED IN THE PAST AND CONTINUE INTO THE PRESENT

1 Mr Greenway *has been using* the new version of RAINBOW for about two weeks.

The Present Perfect Progressive (*have/has been using*) is often used to talk about actions that *began in the past and continue into the present*. For example, people often ask questions like the following:

2 How long *have you been living* in San Francisco?
3 How long *have you been studying* English?

You ask these questions only if the person you are talking to still lives in San Francisco or still studies English.

B ACTIONS THAT PERHAPS HAVE TAKEN PLACE AT ANY TIME BETWEEN THE PAST AND THE PRESENT

4 *Have* you ever *been* to San Francisco?
5 *Have* you ever *used* a computer before?

This is called the Present Perfect Simple. It is used here to talk about single actions. There is no idea of 'definite time' here. The word 'ever' means 'at any time in your life'.

C 'FINISHED' AND 'UNFINISHED' ACTIONS BETWEEN PAST AND PRESENT

6 *Have* you *read* this report?

This question really means 'Have you read all the report?' The answer 'Yes, I have' is only true if you have read all the report, and not just part of it.

7 *Have* you *been reading* this report?

This is a very different question from Example 6. The question does *not* necessarily mean 'Have you read all of the report?' You can honestly say 'Yes, I have' even if you have read only part of it.

8 Robert *has read* the report.

This means 'and now he has finished it' or 'He has read all of it'. We know that at some point in the past – probably the recent past – he finished the report, but we don't know exactly when.

9 Robert *has been reading* the report.

Perhaps Robert has read part of it. Perhaps he has read all of it. The sentence doesn't tell us this. Perhaps he stopped only a few minutes ago.

EXERCISE 3 (ANSWERS PAGE 128)

Use the words or phrases (A–F) to complete the sentences.

A have read	B has ever read	C have been reading
D has read	E read	F has been reading

1 Robert ___ the report for three hours but he hasn't finished it.
2 Robert ___ the report for about two hours yesterday.
3 Robert ___ the report now – every word of it.
4 Robert and Larry ___ the report for about an hour but haven't finished yet.
5 Robert and Larry ___ all of the report now.
6 Do you think Robert ___ a long report like this before?

4 LENGTH & POINT OF TIME

A 'FOR', 'SINCE' OR 'AGO'?

1 We've been using RAINBOW 3 *for* about two weeks.

We use 'for' to talk about 'how long' – and we use it only when we mention the *length of time* – the number of minutes, hours, days, weeks or years we have been doing something.

2 GCS has been in business *since* 1979.

We use 'since' when we mention the *point of time* when something began. Compare the use of 'for' and 'since' in Examples 3 and 4.

3 I've been learning English *for* more than five years.
4 I've been learning English *since* 1997.

'Five years' is a *length of time*. '1997' is a *point of time* at which something began.

5 This company used RAINBOW *for* about five years.

This means that the company no longer uses RAINBOW. The example tells you the length of time that the company used the software; for example, perhaps between the beginning of 1994 and the beginning of 1999.

6 This company used RAINBOW five years *ago*.

Example 6 above tells you only *when* the company used RAINBOW – five years before the present. It does *not* tell you how long the company used it. In other words, if someone said this sentence in the year 2000, it means that the company used RAINBOW in the year 1995 – and probably only in that year. We don't know if the company used it for months or only a few days. The sentence tells us only that the company used the software some time in the year 1995.

B 'AT', 'IN', 'ON' (WITH TIME)

1 We start work here *at* 8 o'clock.

Use 'at' when you mention the exact time of day (clock time).

2 We start work a little later *in* the winter.

Use 'in' when you mention the season (spring, summer, autumn, winter) or the month (January, February, etc.).

3 We don't work here *on* Sunday.

Use 'on' when you mention the day of the week.

EXERCISE 4 (ANSWERS PAGE 128)

Complete the sentences below with 'for', 'since', 'ago' or 'at', 'in' 'on'.

1 I've been waiting for the bus ___ 9.30 and it still hasn't come.
2 I've been waiting for the bus ___ more than forty-five minutes and it still hasn't come.
3 But the bus came fifty minutes ___. Didn't you know?
4 The bus service is much worse ___ Saturday and Sunday.
5 I don't mind waiting ___ the summer, when it's warm.
6 The next bus will come ___ 10.25.

5 INDIRECT QUESTIONS

A IMPORTANT DIFFERENCE IN WORD ORDER

There is an important difference in word order between 'direct questions' (1, 2, 3 below) and 'indirect questions' (A, B, C).

1 **Where *is* the station?**
A **Can you tell me where the station *is*?**

2 **Who *are* those men?**
B **Have you any idea who those men *are*?**

3 **What *does* this word *mean*?**
C **Do you know what this word means?**

B USES OF INDIRECT QUESTIONS

Examples 1, 2, 3 above are very 'direct'. You ask such questions when you are sure the person you are asking knows the answer. Examples A, B, C are 'indirect'. You ask them either because *you aren't sure* if the person you are asking knows the answer, or because you think it is *more polite* to make the question indirect.

4 **How old *are* you?**

This question is very direct; perhaps too direct, especially if you are talking to an older person.

D **Excuse me, but could I ask you how old *you are*?**

This is more polite because you ask for permission to ask the question before you ask it.

5 **Where *were* you yesterday?**

This is too direct in most situations. Even a tough detective like Kovalski sometimes asks this question more politely.

E **Can you tell me where *you were* yesterday?**

Indirect questions are often used when you want someone's opinion. Who really knows the answer to a question like Example 6 below?

6 **Is it going to rain tomorrow?**

It is far easier to answer question F.

F **Do you think *it's going to rain* tomorrow?**

EXERCISE 5 (ANSWERS PAGE 128)

Use phrases A–J to complete questions 1–10.

A	time it is	F	the weather is going
B	does this machine	G	does this book cost
C	is the weather going	H	can Mr Keller see
D	this book costs	I	time is it
E	this machine works	J	Mr Keller can see

1 Can you tell me how much ___ ?
2 How much ___ ?
3 Do you know when ___ me?
4 When ___ me?
5 Could you explain how ___ ?
6 How ___ work?
7 Do you know what ___ in New York now?
8 What ___ in New York now?
9 What do you think ___ to be like tomorrow?
10 What ___ to be like tomorrow?

---

6 POLITE QUESTIONS AND ANSWERS

A ASKING FOR PERMISSION

Questions beginning with 'Do you mind if I . . . ?' are often used in English to ask for permission to do something.

1 *Do you mind if I use your phone?*

A more formal and even more polite variation of this question is:

2 *Would you mind if I used your phone?*

B POLITE ANSWERS TO SUCH QUESTIONS

Notice B's answers in the two short conversations below.

A **Do you mind if I open the window?**
B *No. Go ahead.*

A **Do you mind if I look at your dictionary?**
B *Uh, well, I'm using it myself.*

The polite answer to A's first question is 'No'. This is a short way of saying 'No, I don't mind if you open the window'. In the second conversation, the direct answer would be 'Yes', with the meaning 'Yes, I mind if you use my dictionary'. But it is never polite to answer so directly, so B gives an indirect answer. Here is another example:

A **Do you mind if I open the window.**
B **Well, it's very cold in this room.**

C THE SAME WORD ORDER AS IN INDIRECT QUESTIONS

Notice that when polite questions like these are used to get information, the word order is the same as the indirect questions A–F in Section 5.

3 **Do you mind if I ask you where *you were* yesterday?** (Direct question: **Where *were* you yesterday?**)

4 **Would you mind telling me where *you went* after you left the office?** (Direct question: **Where did *you go* after you left the office?**)

Notice the difference between a direct question and the same question that begins with 'Do you remember . . . ?'

5 **Do you remember *what you did* after you left the office?** (Direct question: **What *did you do* after you left the office?**)

EXERCISE 6 (ANSWERS PAGE 128)

Complete the second question in each pair.

1 *Can I sit here?*
  Do you mind ___ here?
2 *Can I look at your passport?*
  Would you mind ___ your passport?
3 *Where did you buy that hat?*
  Do you remember where ___ that hat?
4 *How much did it cost?*
  Do you also remember how much ___ ?
5 *Why do you want to know?*
  Would you mind telling me ___ to know?
6 *I mean, why are you asking me all these personal questions?*
  Do you mind if I ask you why ___ these personal questions?

7 ACTIVE AND PASSIVE

A EXAMPLES OF 'ACTIVE' AND 'PASSIVE' SENTENCES

1 **Hellman *pushed* someone out of the window.**

This is an 'active' sentence. Hellman is the person who pushed another person out of the window. Hellman didn't fall. Someone else fell. Compare this with Example 2:

2 **Hellman *was* pushed out of the window.**

This is an example of a 'passive' sentence. It means that someone pushed Hellman out of the window. We call such sentences 'passive' because the subject (Hellman) was not the person who did something. *Someone did something to Hellman.*

B USES OF THE PASSIVE

3 **The suicide note *was written* on Hellman's computer.**

We often use passive sentences in English when we don't know who does or did something, or when we don't think it is important to mention the person who does or did something.

In Example 3, above, we don't know who wrote the suicide note, or we don't think it is important to mention the person who wrote the note.

In the conversation in Unit 6, Kovalski asks Ferrante the following question about the suicide cases he has had:

4 **How often *were* suicide notes *left* behind?**

Kovalski uses the passive in Example 4 because it is much easier and shorter to say it this way, and not to mention the people who left the suicide notes behind.

When we want to mention the person who does or did something in a passive sentence, we use 'by'.

5 **Perhaps Hellman was killed *by* someone who works at GCS.**

We often mention the most important information last – at the end of a sentence and not at the beginning. In Example 5 above, the most important part of the sentence is not 'Hellman was killed' but 'by someone who works at GCS'. Compare the two questions in Examples 6 and 7.

6 **Did Hellman write this note?**
7 **Was this note *written* by Hellman?**

In Example 6 (active), perhaps the note is more important than Hellman. Perhaps the speaker really means 'We know that Hellman wrote some notes, but did he also write *this* note?' In Example 7, the really important part of the question is 'by Hellman?' (or perhaps by someone else).

EXERCISE 7 (ANSWERS PAGE 128)

Connect the two parts of each question.

1	Do you think Hellman	A	find the killer?
2	Or was he	B	is found?
3	If he didn't jump, was	C	be found?
4	If so, who	D	killed himself?
5	Can Kovalski ever	E	will she find him?
6	Will the killer ever	F	killed?
7	If so, how	G	pushed him?
8	What will happen when the killer	H	he pushed?

---

8 TWO WAYS OF TALKING ABOUT THE FUTURE

A 'GOING TO' FOR INTENTIONS

1 **Robert is *going to be* in London for three days.**
2 **He's *going to leave* on Friday.**

Examples 1 and 2 tell us about Robert's *intentions*. In English, when we talk about our intentions or other people's intentions, we usually use 'going to'.

B 'AM/IS/ARE –ING' FOR THE ARRANGED FUTURE

3 **I *am staying* in London for three days.**
4 **I *am leaving* on Friday.**

When you have made an arrangement to do something – for example, when you have booked a room at a hotel, or have bought a ticket to go somewhere, you can use the Present Progressive to talk about the future.

5 **What *are* you *doing* tomorrow?**

This question usually means 'Have you made any plans for tomorrow? Is anything already arranged?'

6 **What *are* you *going to do* tomorrow?**

This question usually means 'What do you intend to do tomorrow?'

C 'GOING TO' FOR THINGS THAT CAN'T BE ARRANGED

Imagine you are at home, looking out of a window at the rain. You want to go out – but not in the rain. In this situation, most English speakers ask each other this question:

7 **Do you think it's *going to stop* soon?**

You can't say 'is stopping' in this situation, for a simple reason: it isn't possible to plan or arrange the weather.

EXERCISE 8 (ANSWERS PAGE 128)

Choose the correct way or ways to complete each sentence. Sometimes *both* choices are correct.

1 Do you think it ___ tomorrow?
   A is raining   B is going to rain

2 Do you know what you're ___ tomorrow?
   A going to do   B doing

3 I have to take an examination tomorrow. I hope I'm ___ .
   A passing   B going to pass

4 Robert's boss, Larry Knowles, has a young girlfriend. People say that she's ___ a baby soon.
   A having   B going to have

5 What do you think Larry's wife is ___ when she finds out?
   A going to do   B doing

6 Ladies and gentleman. This is your pilot speaking. We're ___ off in a few minutes.
   A taking   B going to take

7 Germany and England ___ this evening in the World Cup.
   A are playing   B are going to play

8 Which team do you think ___ this evening?
   A is winning   B is going to win

9 ANOTHER WAY OF TALKING ABOUT THE FUTURE

A USING 'WILL' TO TALK ABOUT DECISIONS

1 What'll you have? Tea or coffee?

When someone asks you a question like this, that person is asking you to make a decision. Tea or coffee?

2 I think I'll have coffee, please.

This sounds like a definite decision – and the speaker has just made it. Compare this with Example 3.

3 I think I'm going to have coffee.

Somehow, this doesn't sound as definite. Perhaps the speaker still has not made a final decision.

B 'WILL' FOR PROMISES AND OFFERS OF HELP

4 I'll be at the airport to meet you.

This is a *promise*. The speaker is saying 'You can be sure that I will be at the airport when you arrive.'

5 Just a moment. I'll open the door for you.

If someone says this to you, you can say 'Thank you very much,' or 'That isn't necessary. I can do it myself.' In other words, the other person has offered to help you, and you can either accept the help or say that it isn't necessary.

C 'WILL' FOR PREDICTIONS

When you predict something, you say what you think is going to happen in the future.

6 Do you think this rain will stop soon?

When you ask this question, you are asking someone to predict the future. People use both 'will' and 'going to' when they make predictions, or ask other people to make them.

7 Do you think this rain is going to stop soon?

EXERCISE 9 (ANSWERS PAGE 128)

Choose the correct answer. Sometimes – but not always – two choices or even all three choices are correct.

1 It's warm today but I think ___ colder tomorrow.
   A it'll get   B It's going to get   C It's getting

2 What are your plans for tomorrow? I mean, what ___?
   A will you do   B are you going to do   C are you doing

3 A few years ago, a young man fell in love with Ros Kovalski. One day he asked her a question. '___ marry me?'
   A Will you   B Are you going to   C Do you

4 Ladies and gentlemen. This is your pilot speaking. ___ off in about three minutes.
   A We'll take   B We're taking   C We're going to take

5 Do you know how long Robert Keller ___ in London?
   A will stay   B is staying   C is going to stay

6 I hope ___ the examination tomorrow.
   A I'll pass   B I'm passing   C I'm going to pass

7 Can you lend me some money? ___ it back to you next week.
   A I'm giving   B I'll give   C I'm going to give

---

10 THE 'FUTURE IN THE PAST'

A 'WAS/WERE GOING TO . . .' FOR CHANGES OF PLAN

1 I was going to leave the day after tomorrow.

This suggests very strongly that you have changed your plans.

2 We were going to have a party next Saturday, but . . .

When someone says this, you know how the sentence is going to end before you hear the rest of it. (There is no longer going to be a party next Saturday.) We call this 'the future in the past' because it is no longer the future. The party is cancelled.

B 'WOULD'

3 A lot of people knew that Tom Hellman had personal problems but nobody thought he would kill himself.

You can also say 'was going to' here. This is a slightly different form of the 'future in the past'. We use it to talk about things we didn't know were going to happen. We look back from the present to the past, and talk about what was the future at that time in the past.

4 When I looked out of the window this morning, I thought the weather was going to be nice today. But now look at it. It's raining.

Here, the speaker is looking back at the morning. Perhaps it is the afternoon, or even the evening now. The speaker is talking about 'the future in the past' – what he or she hoped or thought the weather was going to be like later in the day.

EXERCISE 10 (ANSWERS PAGE 128)

Connect the first part of each sentence (1–8) with the second part (A–H).

1 I think I'm going to be in Paris for a week,
2 I thought I was going to be in Paris for a week,
3 When Tom Hellman came to San Francisco, he was very happy and he thought
4 Sergeant Kovalski thinks someone pushed Hellman out of the window and
5 Her boss, Steve Ferrante, didn't know that
6 When you got up this morning, what did you think the weather
7 What do you think the weather
8 Last week, Robert Keller thought he

A his wife and daughter would be happy there, too.
B was going to spend four days in London, but then he had to change his plans.
C was going to be like later?
D but now I've changed my plans.
E she's going to try to find out who did it.
F is going to be like later?
G but perhaps I'll stay longer.
H she was going to spend so much time on the case.

11 RELATIVE PRONOUNS 'THAT', 'WHO', 'WHICH'

A JOINING TWO SENTENCES TOGETHER WITH 'THAT', 'WHO' OR 'WHICH'

Relative pronouns help you to make two sentences into one. For example:

1 A **There's a shop around the corner. It sells computers.**
  B **There's a shop around the corner *that* sells computers.**

2 A **I have a friend. He works there.**
  B **I have a friend *that* works there.**

Notice that in Example 1B, 'that' refers to a *thing* (a shop) and in Example 2B 'that' refers to a *person* (a friend). Both of these sentences are informal and typical of the kind of English people use every day.

B 'WHO' AND 'WHICH' – ESPECIALLY IN MORE FORMAL STYLES OF ENGLISH

The relative pronoun 'that' can be used for *things* or *people*. 'Who' and 'which' are also used as pronouns. However, 'who' refers only to *people* and 'which' refers only to *things*.

3 **Romeo and Juliet is a story about two young people *who* lived in Verona.**

4 **I am going to tell you a story about something *which* happened many years ago.**

Examples 3 and 4 are more formal than Examples 1B and 2B. 'Who' and 'which' are used more often than 'that' in sentences that are formal.

Notice that the relative pronoun 'that' cannot be used after a preposition. The following is therefore not possible:

* The town in ~~that~~ I live . . .

EXERCISE 11A (ANSWERS PAGE 128)

First, complete each sentence below, using only 'who' or 'which'.

1 Global Computer Systems is an international company ____ makes software.
2 Linda Shawcross manages six people ____ deal with customers' problems.
3 The office in ____ they work is in the centre of London.
4 Robert and Linda are talking about a company in London ____ is using the test version of RAINBOW 3.
5 RAINBOW 3 is a new software program ____ can do many things most other software programs can't do.
6 However, there is another software program ____ does almost the same things.
7 I know someone ____ has used that product.
8 The company in ____ he works makes car parts.

EXERCISE 11B (ANSWERS PAGE 128)

In which sentences above can you use 'that' instead of 'who' or 'which'?

12 JOINING TWO SENTENCES WITHOUT USING RELATIVE PRONOUNS

SUBJECT OR OBJECT?

The 'subject' of a sentence is the person or thing that does something in the sentence. Compare Examples 1 and 2:

1 **All the customers (*that/who*) I have spoken to say the same thing.** ('All the customers' = object; 'I' = subject)

2 **All the customers *that/who* have spoken to me say the same thing.** ('All the customers' = subject; 'me' = object)

In Example 1 you can leave out 'that' or 'who' because they are *object* pronouns (they refer to the *object* 'All the customers').

In Example 2, however, you must use 'that' or 'who' because they are *subject* pronouns (they refer to the *subject* 'All the customers').

EXERCISE 12A (ANSWERS PAGE 128)

Underline the words 'that', 'who' or 'which' only when they *are not necessary* in the sentence.

EXAMPLES
Who is the woman <u>that</u> you were talking to?
Oh, that's a woman who works in my department.

1 Who is the woman that was talking to you?
2 I'm looking for a book that can help me to understand how to use relative pronouns.
3 A relative pronoun is a word which refers to a thing or person mentioned earlier in a sentence.
4 I think this is the book that you are looking for.
5 How many relative pronouns are there in the sentences that you have read in this exercise?
6 Sergeant Ros Kovalski is the detective who was here yesterday.
7 Was she the detective that Ed Bondy didn't want to talk to?
8 Was there anybody else that didn't want to talk to her?
9 Was there anybody else that she didn't want to talk to?

EXERCISE 12B (ANSWERS PAGE 128)

Answer 'Yes' or 'No'.

1 Can you use 'who' for things?
2 Can you use 'who' for people?
3 Can you use 'which' for things?
4 Can you use 'which' for people?
5 Can you use 'that' for people?
6 Can you use 'that' for things?
7 Is 'that' used more often in informal sentences than 'which' or 'who'?
8 Is it possible to leave out 'that' or 'which' in the sentence below?

I didn't understand the rules that/which I've just read.

9 Is it possible to leave out 'that' or 'who' in the next sentence?

I didn't understand the person that/who phoned me yesterday.

13 WANT SOMEONE TO DO IT

A WHO IS GOING TO DO IT?

1 **Larry wants to read the report.**
2 **Larry *wants Robert to read* the report.**

In Example 1, Larry is probably going to read the report. In Example 2, Robert is probably going to read it.

3 **Larry gave Robert the report because he *wants him to read* it.**

Notice that in Example 3, 'him' refers to Robert.

4 **Larry didn't understand something his wife said. He wants *her* to explain it.**

In Example 4, 'her' refers to Larry's wife. In other words, in English we often use object pronouns (*me, him, her, us, them*) as the subject of infinitive verbs ('to read', 'to explain', 'to do', etc.). Remember again that the subject is the person or thing that does, did or is going to do something in a sentence.

B VERBS WITH OBJECT + INFINITIVE

Only a few verbs in English are used before object + infinitives. Here are some of those that are most frequently used.

5 **Larry *asked me to read* the report.**
6 **Our teacher *told us to come* earlier than usual on Monday.**
7 **Robert's plane has been delayed. We *expect him to arrive* an hour late.**
8 **We have some new neighbours. We're going to *invite them to come* over tomorrow.**
9 **If you ever go to London in November or December, I'd *advise you to take* an umbrella and a raincoat.**

EXERCISE 13 (ANSWERS ON PAGE 128)

Choose the correct way to complete each sentence.

1 Why does Larry want ___ the report?
  A that Robert reads   B Robert to read
  C Robert is reading

2 Why does he want ___ his travel arrangements?
  A for him to change   B that he changes
  C him to change

3 Robert is going to phone Sue O'Brian and ask ___ change his hotel reservation.
  A she will   B that she will   C her to

4 Do you think Robert expects ___ at the airport when he arrives?
  A her to be   B that she is   C she to be

5 'Would you like ___ you at the airport?' she asked him.
  A I am meeting   B me to meet   C that I will meet

6 'No, I don't think ___ necessary,' he told her.
  A that to be   B that will be   C that being

7 Sue told Robert that it was very cold in London and advised ___ a sweater and other warm clothes with him.
  A he would bring   B he will bring   C him to bring

8 'Would you advise ___ an umbrella, too?' he asked her.
  A me to bring   B me that I will bring
  C that I am bringing

14 'IN ORDER TO', 'SO THAT', ETC.

A WHY ARE THERE CAMERAS IN THE CORRIDOR?

1 **We have cameras in every corridor *in order to* keep a check on visitors.**
2 **We have cameras in every corridor *so that we can* keep a check on visitors.**

Both Examples 1 and 2 tell us why the cameras are there. Very often, the words 'in order' are left out, as in Example 3.

3 **The cameras are there *to keep* a check on visitors.**

B AN IMPORTANT DIFFERENCE BETWEEN 'IN ORDER TO' AND 'SO THAT'

When you use 'in order to', or just 'to', the subject of both parts of the sentence is always the same.

4 ***Kovalski* went to the GCS building *in order to talk/to talk* to the head of security.**

Notice in Example 4 that it is *Kovalski* who went to the GCS building and also *Kovalski* who wanted to talk to the head of security. Compare this with Example 5.

5 **The receptionist always records the time each visitor arrives and leaves *so that we* can see how long they were in the building.**

In Example 5, the subject of the two parts of the sentence is not the same. In the first part 'The receptionist' is the subject. In the second part 'we' is the subject.

6 **Kovalski went there *to ask* Mr Tucker a few questions.**
7 **She went there *so that she could ask* Mr Tucker a few questions.**

In Examples 1, 3, 4 and 6, ('in order to . . .' or 'to . . .') there can be only one subject ('We' in 1, 'The cameras' in 3, and 'Kovalski' in 4 and 6). However, in the examples with 'so that . . .', there can be either one or two subjects ('We' and 'we' in 2, 'The receptionist' and 'we' in 5, 'She' and 'she' in 7).

EXERCISE 14 (ANSWERS ON PAGE 128)

Choose A or B to complete each sentence.

  A in order to   B so that

1 Both our parents worked hard ___ give us a good education.
2 Both our parents worked hard ___ we could have a good education.
3 It's a good idea to buy a good dictionary ___ you can look up the meanings of words you don't understand.
4 I bought this dictionary ___ look up words I don't understand.
5 Visitors to the building all wear a badge ___ we can see who they are and when they came into the building.
6 On the day Hellman died, two men in uniform came into the building ___ deliver one small package.
7 Why do you need two men ___ deliver one small package?
8 Kovalski went to see Bondy in his office ___ she could study him closely.
9 We want you to do this exercise ___ you can get a better idea of a small but important difference between 'in order to' and 'so that'.

15 MORE WAYS OF EXPLAINING 'WHY'

Examples 1–4 show other ways of explaining why you are doing something.

1   I'm phoning you now *because* I have something very important to tell you.

2   *The reason* I'm phoning is that I have something very important to tell you.

3   I have something very important to tell you. *That's why* I'm phoning now.

4   I have something very important to tell you. *So* I decided to phone you.

Example 1 shows the simplest way of explaining the reason for doing something. But notice the difference between Examples 1 and 2. The words 'The reason' at the beginning of Example 2 immediately tell the listener that you want to explain something. Those words are a signal that means 'Please listen carefully'.

In Example 3, the words 'That's why' tell the listener 'Please think back to what I said a moment ago and you will understand why I am phoning now.'

The word 'So' in Example 4 is also a 'backward looking' word. It tells the listener that you have already mentioned the reason you did or are doing something.

EXERCISE 15 (ANSWERS PAGE 128)

Use the words or phrases (A–F) to complete the sentences below.

A in order to   B That's why   C So
D so that   E The reason   F because

1   Kovalski wanted to talk to the head of security at GCS. ___ she went there yesterday.
2   ___ she wanted to talk to him was to find out more about the company's security arrangements.
3   When she went to his office the door was open. ___ she walked in.
4   The director of security's name was Tucker. Tucker knew she had come ___ talk about security arrangements.
5   He closed the door ___ nobody else could hear what they were talking about.
6   He told her that there were security cameras ___ the company wanted to know who was in the building at any time.
7   'You can look at the videotapes ___ find out who was in the building the morning Hellman died,' he said.
8   ___ she wants to look at the videotapes is to see who was in the building when Hellman died.

16 USING 'IF' TO EXPLAIN 'WHY'

A   I WOULDN'T BE DOING THIS IF . . .

1   I *wouldn't be phoning* now if it *weren't* important.

When Ed Bondy says this in Unit 11, he is explaining *why* he is phoning at midnight, when most people are asleep.

B   'IF' AND THE 'UNREAL PRESENT'

2   If Robert *were* an engineer, he *would understand*.

Example 2 tells us *why* Robert doesn't understand. Robert doesn't understand because he *isn't* an engineer.

C   NOTICE AGAIN THE LINK BETWEEN 'WHY?' AND CONDITIONAL SENTENCES

3   Life *would* be impossible *if I didn't have* a job.
4   I *would* travel all over the world *if I were* rich.
5   Ed Bondy *would* be easier to work with *if he weren't* so arrogant.

Example 3 also tells us *why life isn't impossible* for the speaker. The answer is that the speaker *has a job*.
Example 4 tells us *why the speaker doesn't travel all over the world*. The reason is that the speaker *isn't rich*.
Example 5 tells us *why Ed Bondy isn't easier to work with*. The answer is that he *is so arrogant*.

D   'WOULD' = DISTANCE FROM THE PRESENT

6   I *would like to be* rich.

This means you *aren't* rich. The word *would* here suggests 'distance from the present'; that something is *not* true now but that you *would like it to be true*. Compare with Example 7.

7   I *like being* rich.

This means you *are* rich, and you like it.

E   WHY DO WE USE PAST FORMS (DID, WERE, HAD, ETC.) TO TALK ABOUT THE 'UNREAL PRESENT'?

The verbs used in the 'if' part of the sentence *seem* to be about the past, but they are really about an 'unreal situation now'. One explanation is that the past forms make it clear that the speaker is talking about something *distant* from reality, just as the past is *distant* from the present.

EXERCISE 16 (ANSWERS PAGE 128)

Use past forms in the 'if' part of each sentence below to make it clear that the situation is 'distant from reality'. (Use 'were' and not 'was' to make it even clearer that the situation is 'distant from reality'.)

1   What would you do if you ___ more money?
2   Do you think life would be better for you if you ___ rich?
3   How would you feel if Ed Bondy ___ your boss?
4   You don't know Ed Bondy, of course, but do you think you would like him if you ___ him?
5   Do you see the sun every day? How would you feel if you never ___ it again?
6   You don't live in San Francisco. Do you think you would be happy if you ___ there?
7   Perhaps more people would buy RAINBOW if it ___ easier to use.

17 TWO KINDS OF 'IF' SENTENCES

A FUTURE & 'UNREAL PRESENT'

1 If Ed *has* more time, he'*ll explain* it to Robert.
2 If Ed *had* more time, he'*d explain* it to Robert.

Example 1 suggests that perhaps Ed *will* explain it to Robert at some time. Example 2 tells us that Ed *isn't* going to explain it to Robert *because* he doesn't have enough time.

3 I'*ll come* and see you tomorrow if I *have* time.
4 I'*d come* and see you tomorrow if I *had* time.

Example 3 is like Example 1. It suggests that perhaps you will come. Example 4, however, is like Example 2. It means that you *aren't* going to come *because* you don't have enough time.

B SHORT FORMS: I'LL, I'D, WON'T, WOULDN'T

Remember that especially in spoken English, short forms are frequently used.

I **will** do it	▶	**I'll** do it
I **would** do it	▶	**I'd** do it
I **will not** do it	▶	I **won't** do it
I **would not** do it	▶	I **wouldn't** do it

C IF ROBERT WERE AN ENGINEER, . . .

5 If Robert *were* an engineer, he *would* understand.

Notice again that the 'if' part of this example gives a *reason* for something. The reason Robert *doesn't* understand is because he *isn't* an engineer.

Some speakers say 'If Robert *were* . . .' and some say 'If Robert *was* . . .'. Both forms are possible.

In all other examples of the 'unreal present', the form of the verb used in the 'if' part of the sentence is exactly the same as the Simple Past.

6 If I *were* rich, I'd stop working.
7 If I *knew* more English, perhaps I'd get a better job.
8 My doctor told me I would feel better if I *didn't drink* so much coffee and I *got* more exercise.

EXERCISE 17 (ANSWERS PAGE 128)

Use the correct form of the verb in brackets to complete each sentence.

EXAMPLES
(*be*) What would you do if you *were* rich?
(*buy*) If I were rich, I *would buy* a big house.

1 (*rain*) What will you do if it ___ tomorrow?
2 (*not come*) We'll get a taxi if the bus ___ soon.
3 (*be*) My life wouldn't be very different if I ___ rich.
4 (*like*) If you knew my friend, you ___ her.
5 (*have*) I don't want a car. I would never use it if I ___ one.
6 (*be*) Would you marry me if I ___ ten years younger?
7 (*be*) You'll understand this when you ___ older, my son.
8 (*stop*) Steve Ferrante would feel better if he ___ smoking.

18 'IF' AND 'WHEN' IN THE FUTURE

A COMPARE THE TWO SENTENCES

1 **When** Bondy finds out about this, he will be very angry.
2 **If** Bondy finds out about this, he will be very angry.

Example 1 ('When . . .') tells us that the speaker is sure Bondy will find out. Example 2 ('If . . .') tells us that the speaker isn't sure about this at all. Perhaps Bondy will find out. Perhaps he won't.

B 'WHEN/IF YOU DO THIS . . . ,' NOT 'WHEN/IF YOU WILL DO THIS . . .'

In Example 2 above, the 'if' part of the sentence contains a *cause* ('If Bondy finds out about this') and the other part of the sentence contains a *result* ('he will be very angry').

3 If we *have* enough money next year, we'*ll buy* a new car.
4 When I *see* you tomorrow, I'*ll give* you the documents.

In Examples 3 and 4, the verbs (*have, see*) after 'If' or 'When' are in the *present* form, and not the future form (*will have/will see*). This is normal in English. The verb in the part of the sentence that contains a *cause* or *reason* for something is in the present.

C 'I WONDER IF . . . ', 'DO YOU KNOW IF . . . ?'

5 I wonder *if it's going to* rain tomorrow.
6 Do you know *if you'll* be able to come to the party?

In Examples 5 and 6, the 'if' parts of the sentences *do not* tell us *why* something will happen or is going to happen.

In Example 5, 'I wonder' means 'I'd like to know'.

Example 6 is a *request for information*. (See Sections 5 and 6, page 115, on direct and indirect questions.) In sentences like this, some form of the future is often used after 'if' or 'when'.

EXERCISE 18 (ANSWERS PAGE 128)

Choose the correct word or phrase, A or B, to complete gaps 1–8 in the text below about Ed Bondy.

1 A if	B when		**5** A if	B when		
2 A if	B when		**6** A will sleep	B sleep		
3 A will drink	B drink		**7** A I'll sleep	B I sleep		
4 A if	B when		**8** A I'll feel	B I feel		

Ed Bondy hasn't been sleeping very well lately. Perhaps that's why he feels so tired **1** ___ he wakes up in the morning. His doctor has told him he will sleep far better **2** ___ he doesn't drink so much coffee.

'You drink far too much coffee. I'm sure you'll sleep better if you **3** ___ less coffee. I think you'll sleep even better **4** ___ you don't drink any coffee after three in the afternoon. I'm going to give you some tablets. Take one tonight, **5** ___ you go to bed. If you **6** ___ badly tonight, take two tablets tomorrow night,' the doctor said.

Ed is getting ready for bed now and has just taken a tablet. 'I wonder if **7** ___ well tonight. If I sleep at least seven hours without waking up, **8** ___ all right tomorrow morning,' he is thinking.

19 'CAN' AND 'COULD'

A 'CAN YOU . . . ?' (IS IT POSSIBLE FOR YOU TO . . . ?)

1 *Can* you hear me?
2 *Can* you read these numbers without your glasses?

This is one of the most frequent uses of 'can' in English. Here, the meaning is 'Is it possible for you to do this?'

B SPECIAL KNOWLEDGE OR SPECIAL ABILITY

3 *Can* you play the piano?
4 How many languages *can* you speak?

In Examples 3 and 4, 'can' really means 'Do you *know how* to do this?'

C THE PAST FORM OF 'CAN'

5 RAINBOW 3 does far more things than RAINBOW 2 *could* do.
6 I *couldn't* read those numbers yesterday without my glasses.
7 Mozart *could* play the piano and violin when he was four years old.

In Examples 5, 6 and 7, 'could' (or 'couldn't') is simply the past form of 'can', in the sense of 'ability, possibility or special knowledge in the past'.

D THE 'POLITE' USE OF 'CAN' AND 'COULD' IN THE PRESENT

8 *Can/Could* you tell me where the station is?
9 *Can/Could* we postpone the meeting?

In Examples 8 and 9, 'can' and 'could' are both polite ways of asking people to do something in the present or future. There is very little difference of meaning between them. In other words, 'could' loses its past meaning here and is just another way of saying 'Please do this'.

EXERCISE 19 (ANSWERS PAGE 128)

Complete the sentences below with 'can' or 'could'. In three – and only three – of these sentences, it is possible to use *either* 'can' or could'.

1 Let's see how good your eye-sight is. ___ you read these letters without your glasses? Is it possible?
2 Only a few years ago, I ___ read without glasses, but it isn't possible any more.
3 When I was younger, I ___ walk very long distances, but now I get tired very quickly.
4 Pardon? What did you say? ___ you repeat that, please?
5 There's a word here I don't understand. ___ you explain it to me, please?
6 There's an article in the newspaper about a little girl She's only three years old but she ___ already read and write three foreign languages.
7 We climbed to the top of the mountain yesterday and we ___ see the city far away in the distance.
8 Oh, I see. Mr Bondy isn't there. Well, ___ I leave a message for him?
9 When Mozart was four, he ___ play the violin and piano.

20 'COULDN'T HAVE DONE', 'MUST BE', 'MUST HAVE BEEN'

A 'COULDN'T HAVE DONE IT' = IT ISN'T POSSIBLE THAT THIS HAPPENED

1 Bondy *couldn't have killed* Hellman. He was checking in at the airport when Hellman died.
2 The students couldn't have done the exercise. It isn't in the book they're using at the moment.

Examples 1 and 2 mean 'I don't believe this happened. It just isn't possible.'

B 'MUST BE' = I'M SURE IT IS TRUE; 'MAY BE' = PERHAPS IT IS TRUE

3 You *must be* very tired.
4 I've never been to Paris but it *must be* very beautiful.

Examples 3 and 4 tell us that the speaker doesn't really know but is still sure that something is true.

5 It *may be* a coincidence, but there *must* be another explanation.

When Silvina says the sentence above in Unit 16, she means 'Perhaps it is a coincidence, but I'm sure there is another explanation'.

C 'MUST HAVE BEEN TRUE' = I'M SURE IT WAS TRUE

6 The problem *must have been* very serious.
7 Cleopatra *must have been* very beautiful.

In Examples 6 and 7 the speakers do not know but are still sure that 'the problem was very serious' and that 'Cleopatra was very beautiful'.

EXERCISE 20 (ANSWERS PAGE 128)

Each sentence in the first group (1–8) belongs with one sentence from the second group (A–H). Connect the two 'partners' by writing the letters after each number.

1 __ 2 __ 3 __ 4 __ 5 __ 6 __ 7 __ 8 __

1 I'm sorry you couldn't phone me yesterday.
2 You couldn't have phoned me yesterday.
3 Robert has just come home after working twelve hours.
4 Last Friday, Robert worked twelve hours.
5 Ed Bondy must have loved his mother very much.
6 Ed Bondy must love his mother very much.
7 One restaurant was very crowded.
8 The next restaurant was almost empty.

A He was terribly sad and unhappy when she died.
B He must have been very tired when he got home.
C I was at home all the time and the phone never rang.
D We wanted to eat there but we couldn't find a table.
E I know you wanted to phone but I suppose you were far too busy.
F He goes to visit her every week and always buys her flowers.
G He must be very tired.
H We could have found a table but we didn't want to eat there.

21 'MUST DO', 'SHOULD DO' AND 'SHOULD HAVE DONE'

A 'MUST DO' AND 'SHOULD DO'

1 You *must tell* Larry about this.

2 All visitors *must go* to reception on entering the building.

As we have seen in Section 20 (see page 122) you can use 'must' when you are sure something is true. You can also use 'must' to give special emphasis to something. Example 1 suggests that the speaker is very worried about something, and thinks it is essential to tell Larry about it. Example 2 is very formal. It could be a written notice at the entrance to a large office building with strict security.

3 You *should tell* Larry about this.

4 You *should go* to reception when you come into the building. Tell them you have an appointment with me.

Example 3 is *advice*, not an order or command. Example 4 is far less formal than Example 2. You could say this to someone who is coming to visit you at work.

B 'SHOULD DO' AND 'SHOULD HAVE DONE'

5 There's something I *should tell* you.

This is a very good way to get someone's attention. It suggests that the speaker feels some kind of obligation, or even a moral duty to give you some very important information.

6 There's something I *should have told* you.

This means 'I didn't tell you about this earlier and I'm sorry I didn't.'

7 You *should have seen* Ed's face when Robert told him that customers don't like RAINBOW 3.

This means 'I'm sorry you didn't see Ed's face.' It refers to what is sometimes called 'the unreal past' (see Section 26, page 125) – situations that never happened, as in Example 8.

8 You *should have been* here at 8.30. You're an hour late!

This clearly means 'You didn't come at 8.30. You knew that you should be here at that time. You didn't do what you should have done.'

EXERCISE 21 (ANSWERS PAGE 128)

Each sentence in the first group (1–5) belongs with one sentence from the second group (A–E). Connect the two 'partners' by writing the letters after each number.

1 __   2 __   3 __   4 __   5 __

1 You must tell Larry about this.
2 You should tell Larry about this.
3 You should have told Larry about this.
4 You must have told Larry about this.
5 You shouldn't have told Larry about this.

A Someone told him and you are the only person it could have been. So, if you didn't tell him, who did?
B He would probably be very interested if he heard what you've just told me.
C He has enough problems already and now that you've told him, he'll be even more worried than he was before.
D It's a very serious problem and he is the only person who can solve it.
E I can't understand why you didn't tell him.

22 'MAY', 'MUST', 'WOULD BE –ING'

A 'IT MAY HAPPEN' AND 'IT MAY BE HAPPENING'

1 Someone in this company *may be giving* DS information about RAINBOW.

This is a statement about the *present*. When Silvina says this to Robert in Unit 16, she means 'Perhaps someone *is giving* DS information'. Compare this with Example 2.

2 Someone *may give* DS information.

This is a statement about the *future*, not the present. It means 'Perhaps someone *will give* DS information'.

3 You *may be making* a big mistake!

Perhaps the person you are speaking to has already started something that you think is a big mistake, but there is just enough time to stop now, before it is too late. The act is still unfinished.

B WOULD BE –ING

Compare Examples 1 and 3 above with an example you saw in Unit 11 and in Section 16 (See page 120).

4 Ed *wouldn't be phoning* now if it weren't important.

The progressive form (*be –ing*) in Examples 1, 3 and 4 always suggests that there is something *unfinished*. Example 4 means that Ed is phoning at this minute and has not finished yet.

C MUST BE –ING

5 Someone *must be giving* DS information about our plans.

The speaker is sure that someone has given DS information before and will do so again. In both Examples 1 and 5, the speaker is talking about a *series* of acts. In both examples, the series is *unfinished*.

EXERCISE 22 (ANSWERS PAGE 128)

Choose the correct way, A or B, to complete the second sentence in each pair.

1 DS is getting information about our plans. Someone in our company may ___ them this information.
   A sell   B be selling

2 Stop what you are doing. Think again! You may ___ a serious mistake!
   A make   B be making

3 I can hear people next door singing and laughing. They must ___ a party
   A have   B be having

4 It's your birthday next week. We must ___ a party.
   A have   B be having

5 The sun is shining now but I can see dark clouds, too. It may ___ soon.
   A rain   B be raining

6 I don't have enough money to buy a new car. I would ___ one if I had more money.
   A buy   B be buying

7 Nobody is sitting in the park because it is raining. If the sun were shining, a lot of people would ___ there now.
   A sit   B be sitting

23 'UNLESS' AND 'UNTIL'

A UNLESS IT HAPPENS

1 **I'll never find out if Bondy did it *unless* you *give* me another day.**

Kovalski says this to Steve Ferrante in Unit 17. Exactly the same meaning can be expressed with 'if not', as in Example 2:

2 **I'll never find out *if* you *don't give* me another day.**

In other words, the negative idea is already in the word 'unless' in Example 1.

3 **Ferrante thinks that Kovalski will never solve her other cases *unless* he *turns* the Hellman case over to the FBI.**

Example 3 uses 'unless'. Exactly the same idea can be expressed with 'if not', as in Example 4.

4 **Ferrante thinks that Kovalski will never solve her other cases *if* he *doesn't turn* the Hellman case over to the FBI.**

This explains the difference in meaning between the two questions in Examples 5 and 6.

5 **What does Ferrante think will happen *if* he *turns* the Hellman case over to the FBI?**

ANSWER: He thinks Kovalski *will have more time to solve* all the other cases she is working on.

6 **What does Ferrante think will happen *unless* he *turns* the Hellman case over to the FBI?**

ANSWER: He thinks Kovalski *will never solve* all the other cases she is working on.

B UNTIL NINE/UNTIL **I** COME BACK

7 **The shops here are open *until* nine.**

Example 7 means that the shops close at nine. They stay open *up to* nine o'clock. 'Until' means 'up to the point of time that is mentioned'.

8 **Wait here *until* I come back.**

When 'until' is used to connect two actions ('wait' and 'come back'), the verb that comes after 'until' is always in the present, never the future. (Never say: * Wait here until I ~~will~~ come back.)

EXERCISE 23 (ANSWERS PAGE 128)

Complete sentences 1–8 about things parents often say to their children. Use the six words and phrases (A–F). (*Two words or phrases can each be used more than once.*)

A until	**B** unless	**C** don't go
D go	**E** don't	**F** stop

1 You'll never learn anything unless you ___ to school.
2 If you ___ to school, you'll never learn anything.
3 You won't pass your examinations ___ you study.
4 You must stay in school ___ you pass all your examinations.
5 You can watch television this evening ___ nine o'clock.
6 You'll be tired tomorrow unless you ___ watching television now and go to bed.
7 If you ___ stop watching television now, I'll be very angry.
8 I'll be very angry ___ you stop watching television now.

24 INFINITIVE ('TO DO') OR GERUND ('DOING')

A VERB + INFINITIVE CONSTRUCTIONS

Some verbs in English are often followed by an infinitive but *never* by a gerund. Here are some of the most important.

1 **I wouldn't *like to be* out in this weather.**
2 **What do you *want to do* this evening?**
3 **I *need to talk* to you.**
4 **How long do you *plan to stay*?**
5 **They have *arranged to meet* next week.**
6 **We *hope to see* you again soon.**
7 **Robert hopes that Silvina will *decide to accept* the offer.**

B TYPICAL VERB + GERUND CONSTRUCTIONS

There are also a number of verbs which are often followed by a gerund but *never* by an infinitive. Here are some of the most important.

8 **You *keep saying* that. (= You say that again and again)**
9 **How much time do you *spend talking* on the phone every day?**
10 **What is Kovalski going to do after she *finishes talking* to Mr Tucker?**
11 **I *enjoy walking* in the rain.**
12 **Would you *mind waiting* just a few minutes?**

C THREE VERBS THAT CAN BE FOLLOWED BY A GERUND OR AN INFINITIVE WITHOUT A CHANGE OF MEANING

13 **I don't like *being/to be* out in this weather.**
14 **I hate *doing/to do* this.**
15 **It suddenly *began raining/to rain*.**

D 'I WOULDN'T LIKE TO BE . . .'/ 'I DON'T LIKE BEING/TO BE . . .'

Compare Examples 1 and 13 above. Example 1 suggests that you *aren't* outside in bad weather. It is the 'unreal present', and the gerund is *not* used. Example 13, however, suggests that you *are* out in bad weather. There is nothing 'unreal' about this situation, and you can use *either* the infinitive (*to be*) or the gerund (*being*).

EXERCISE 24 (ANSWERS PAGE 128)

What is the correct form of the verb in brackets ( )?
In which two sentences can you use the infinitive or the gerund?

1 Some people enjoy (*do*) ___ exercises like this.
2 Would you like (*do*) ___ another exercise like this?
3 I stopped (*smoke*) ___ a year ago.
4 How much time do you spend (*listen*) ___ to the radio?
5 The company plans (*make*) ___ some important changes.
6 Would you mind (*close*) ___ the window, please?
7 I keep (*make*) ___ the same mistake.
8 I hope (*spend*) ___ a few days in Japan soon.
9 I've arranged (*stay*) ___ at the Tokyo Hilton.
10 Have you finished (*read*) ___ the report yet?
11 No, in fact I haven't even begun (*read*) ___ it yet.
12 I hate (*get up*) ___ early in the winter, when it is dark and cold.

25 'REMEMBER DOING/TO DO' AND 'STOP DOING/TO DO'

A 'REMEMBER DOING' OR 'REMEMBER TO DO'?

1 **Don't you *remember shouting* at me the last time we met?**
2 **Do you *remember meeting* me last year?**

Both examples refer to the *past*. They mean:

(Example 1) You shouted at me the last time we met. Don't you remember that?
(Example 2) We met last year. Do you remember?

In other words 'remember doing' means 'to remember that *you did something in the past*'.

3 **I must *remember to send* my mother some flowers on her birthday.**
4 **Please *remember to turn* off the lights before you leave.**

Both these examples refer to the *future*, not the past. They mean:

(Example 3) I must send my mother some flowers. I must remember that.

(Example 4) Please turn off the lights. Don't forget that when you leave.

In other words, 'remember to do' means 'to remember that you *must do something in the future*'.

B 'STOP DOING' OR 'STOP TO DO'?

5 ***Stop arguing*, Ed.**
6 ***Stop talking* about the weather.**

When you say 'Stop doing that' you mean 'Don't do that any more'.

7 **We've been driving for six hours. Let's *stop to have* something to eat.**
8 **We worked ten hours yesterday. We didn't *stop* even *to have* lunch.**

'Stop to do' something means 'Stop one thing and then do something else'.

EXERCISE 25 (ANSWERS PAGE 128)

Match sentences 1–8 with sentences (A–H) that mean the same thing.

1 Ed should stop listening to Andrea.
2 Ed should stop to listen to Andrea.
3 Let's stop talking about this.
4 Let's stop to talk about this.
5 Robert doesn't remember meeting Silvina.
6 Robert didn't remember to meet Silvina.
7 I didn't remember to turn off the lights.
8 I don't remember turning off the lights.

A This is important. I want to talk about it.
B This is not important. I don't want to talk about it any more.
C I didn't turn off the lights.
D I can't remember if I turned them off or not.
E Ed should listen to Andrea even when he is busy.
F It would be better if he didn't listen to her any more.
G Silvina expected Robert to meet her but he forgot.
H Robert has met Silvina before but he has forgotten.

26 UNREAL PRESENT AND PAST

A UNREAL PRESENT

1 **If a big wave *came*, it *would wash* Danny into the sea.**
2 **If I *won* a million dollars, I'*d* probably *spend* it all.**
3 **If I *were* Danny, I *wouldn't sleep* under the pier.**
4 **If Ed *were* still alive, he *would* probably *make* the same mistake again.**

Notice in Examples 1–4 that the verb in the 'If' part of the sentence is in the *past*, and the verb in the next part of the sentence is always 'would' + infinitive (without 'to').

Sometimes, the term 'unreal present' is a little misleading. Example 1 suggests that the danger is very real. However, the use of the past form 'came' in 'If a big wave *came*, . . .', makes the danger seem less great than in the example below:

If a big waves *comes*, it *will wash* Danny into the sea.

Here, the danger seems much greater than in Example 1. In the same way, Example 2 is not completely unreal. Perhaps the speaker thinks it is possible that he or she will win a million dollars. However, again the use of the past form 'won' in 'If I *won* . . .' suggests that the speaker does not think it is really going to happen. Compare this with the example below:

If I *win* a million dollars, I'*ll spend* it all.

This suggests the speaker thinks it is far more possible that he or she is going to win a million dollars.

B UNREAL PAST

5 **If a big wave *had come*, it *would have washed* Danny away.**
6 **If I *had won* a million dollars last year, I *would* probably *have spent* it all by now.**
7 **If Danny *hadn't slept* under the pier last night, he *would* never *have heard* Andrea and Ed talking.**
8 **If Ed *hadn't gone* to the pier last night, he *would* still *be* alive today.**

Notice that in Examples 5–8, the verb is in the Past Perfect form (*had done*) and in Examples 5-7, the next part of the sentence is 'would' + 'have done'. Examples 5–7 are all 'pure unreal past'. A big wave *didn't come* and wash Danny away (Example 5). The speaker *didn't win* a million dollars last year and for this reason has not spent it all by now (Example 6). Danny heard Andrea and Ed because he *slept* under the pier last night (Example 7).

Example 8 is sometimes called 'mixed unreal past and unreal present'. Ed *went* to the pier last night (past). That's why he *isn't* alive today (present).

EXERCISE 26 (ANSWERS PAGE 128)

Two words are missing from each sentence. What are they?

1 Ed wouldn't ___ gone to the pier if he ___ known about Andrea's plan.
2 What ___ Andrea have done if she ___ known Danny was sleeping under the pier?
3 Do you think Ed would still ___ alive if Andrea had ___ that Danny was under the pier?
4 What ___ you ___ done if you had won $1,000,000 last year?
5 Would you have bought a boat and a big house if you ___ ___ a lot of money last year?

27 'DO IT'/'HAVE IT DONE' AND 'LET SOMEONE DO IT'

A 'DO IT' OR 'HAVE IT DONE'?

1 Andrea *killed* Bondy.
2 Andrea *had* Bondy *killed*.

Example 2 means that *Andrea paid someone to kill Bondy*, and not that she killed him herself.

B 'LET SOMEONE DO IT'

3 I can't *let* you *go* to Portland.
4 *Let* me *do* it.

This construction means 'permit or allow someone to do something'. You cannot use this construction in sentences like the following:

* * Where can I ~~let my hair cut~~?
* * I have to ~~let my car repaired~~.

The correct way to say such sentences is as follows, in Examples 5 and 6.

5 Where can I *have* my hair *cut*?
6 I have to *have* my car *repaired*.

Notice the word order in this construction:

Have + object + *done*

The 'done' form of the verb is the form we use in the Present Perfect:

Have you *repaired* your car yet?

Compare this with Examples 7 and 8.

7 Have you *had* your car *repaired* yet?
8 Yes. I *had* that *done* last week.

EXERCISE 27 (ANSWERS PAGE 128)

Two words are missing from each sentence. What are they?

1 Do you cut your own hair or do you ___ it ___?
2 I usually ___ my hair ___ once every six or seven weeks.
3 I can't clean the carpet myself, so I'm ___ to have it ___.
4 I had a serious problem with my car but now I've ___ it ___ and it runs perfectly now.
5 If I won a million dollars, I wouldn't build a new house myself. I would ___ one ___.
6 Only a specialist can do this job, so I think I'll ___ it ___ by a specialist.
7 Use SPEED DELIVERY SERVICES to ___ things ___ all over the world.
8 Do you make your clothes yourself or do you ___ them ___?

28 'WHO KILLED HIM?' AND 'WHO DID HE KILL?'

A WHO DID IT?

1 *Who did* Bondy *kill*?

Ask this question only if you think Bondy killed someone.

2 *Who killed* Bondy?

This is a very different question. You ask it if you want to know the name of Bondy's killer.

Bondy killed someone. Who? = 'Who did Bondy kill?'
Someone killed Bondy. Who? = 'Who killed Bondy?'

B 'WHY DID SHE DO IT?'/'WHY DID SHE HAVE IT DONE?'

3 Why *did* Andrea *kill* him?

You can ask this question only if you think Andrea was the killer. But we know that she wasn't. So we ask a different question, as in Example 4.

4 Why *did* she *have* him *killed*?

Another way of asking this question is:

Why did she pay someone to kill him?

5 Who *paid* someone *to kill* him?
6 Who *had* him *killed*?

Examples 5 and 6 have the same meaning:

Someone paid someone else to do it . Who was the person who paid someone else? = 'Who had it done?'

EXERCISE 28 (ANSWERS PAGE 128)

Choose the correct way, A, B, C or D, to complete each question below.

1 Who ___ to kill Bondy?
   A paid the hitman   B let the hitman pay
   C pay the hitman   D the hitman paid

2 In other words, who ___?
   A kill Bondy   B has Bondy killed
   C let Bondy kill   D had Bondy killed

3 Did Andrea ___?
   A had killed him   B have him killed
   C him let kill   D has had him killed

4 Who ___ to go to Portland?
   A wants   B does want
   C want   D did want

5 Why ___ to talk to Andrea?
   A does Kovalski want   B wants Kovalski to
   C wanted Kovalski   D do Kovalski want

6 Who ___ Hellman killed?
   A think you had   B do you think had
   C you think has   D you think had

7 Do you think Andrea and Bondy ___?
   A have him killed   B has killed him
   C let kill him   D had him killed

8 Why did they want to ___?
   A let him kill   B have him killed
   C have killed him   D has him killed

29 ASK/TELL SOMEONE TO DO SOMETHING

A ASK SOMEONE TO DO SOMETHING

We use this form to talk about *requests* or *invitations* often after they are made. At the beginning of the conversation between Kovalski and Andrea on page 92, Andrea says this to Kovalski:

1 *Be* as brief as possible.

Later in the same conversation, Andrea says this:

2 I *asked you to be* as brief as possible.

Andrea is talking about the request in Example 1.

Suppose a friend says this to you:

I'm having a party tomorrow. Why don't you come?

This is an invitation. Later, when you talk about it, you can say this:

3 One of my friends has *asked me to come* to a party tomorrow.

B TELL SOMEONE TO DO SOMETHING

We use this form to talk about *orders*, *commands* and *instructions* . For example, a doctor says this to you when you have a very bad cold:

Stay in bed. Keep warm. Drink lots of liquids.

Afterwards, you can say:

4 The doctor *told me to stay* in bed, *to keep* warm and *to drink* lots of liquids.

Or suppose the same friend who invited you to a party said this.

Come at eight o'clock. Don't be late.

You think this is more than just a polite request, so later you say:

5 My friend *told me to come* at eight and *not to be* late.

EXERCISE 29 (ANSWERS PAGE 128)

Kovalski said these things to Andrea. How could you talk about them later, using 'ask' or 'tell'?

EXAMPLE
'Would you mind answering a few questions?'
She asked her to answer a few questions.

1 'Could you come to the police station?'
 She ___ her ___ to the police station.
2 'Come to the police station immediately!'
 She ___ her ___ the police station immediately.
3 'Please tell me a little about your company.'
 She ___ her ___ her a little about her company.
4 'Tell me where you were last Sunday!'
 She ___ her ___ her where she was last Sunday.

30 'IT WOULD BE BETTER/IT WOULD HAVE BEEN BETTER'. 'IF YOU DID/IF YOU WERE'. 'IF YOU HAD DONE/IF YOU HAD BEEN' (MIXED CONDITIONALS)

In English (and in all other languages spoken on this small planet) there are ways of talking about something that really happened in the past and then talking about a result which is very different from the real result.

The *cause* is in the *past* but the *result* is in the *present*.

	PAST (cause)	PRESENT (result)
A	**Ed *went* to the old pier.**	**He *isn't* alive now.**
B	**You *won* a million dollars last year.**	**You *aren't* poor any more.**
C	**You *spent* all the money this year.**	**You *aren't* rich any more.**
D	**You *went* to bed very late last night.**	**You *feel* very tired now.**

Now compare these 'past causes' and 'present results' with examples 1–4 below:

1 If Ed *hadn't gone* to the old pier that night almost a year ago, he *would* still *be* alive today.
2 If you *hadn't won* all that money, you *would* still *be* poor now.
3 If you *hadn't spent* it all, you *would* still *be* rich now.
4 If I *hadn't gone* to bed so late last night, I *wouldn't be* so tired now.

■ When the *cause* is in the *past*, but the *result* is in the *present*, use 'had done' or 'had been' to talk about the real *cause* in the 'If' part of the sentence.

■ Use 'would do' or 'would be' to talk about the unreal *result* – the result that is different from the real result now.

EXERCISE 30 (ANSWERS PAGE 128)

Connect the first part of each sentence (1–6) with the part (A–F) that you think goes with it.

1 You would feel a lot better today
2 If our company hadn't spent so much money last year on the new office building
3 I don't think I would have this terrible cold
4 If I had been born in San Francisco
5 If Shakespeare had never been born
6 What would the world be like now

A if I hadn't gone out in the rain yesterday.
B if the two world wars of 1914–18 and 1939–45 had never happened?
C I would be an American citizen now.
D if you hadn't drunk so much yesterday evening.
E English literature would not be what it is today.
F we would have a lot more money to spend this year.

31 'TAG' QUESTIONS AND ANSWERS

A REPEATING PART OF THE QUESTION IN THE ANSWER

Notice how speaker B uses part of speaker A's question in each answer.

A Excuse me. *Do you speak English?*
B Yes, I *do.*
A *Can you tell me where Post Street is?*
B I'm afraid I *can't.* I don't know the city very well.
A Oh, *are you a stranger here, too?*
B Yes, I *am.*

- If the question begins with 'Do you . . . ?', B can answer 'Yes, I do' or 'No, I don't'.
- If the question begins with 'Can you . . . ?', B can answer 'Yes, I can' or 'No, I can't'.
- If the question begins with 'Are you . . . ?', B can answer 'Yes, I am', or 'No, I'm not'.

EXERCISE 31A (ANSWERS OPPOSITE)

Match each question (1–6) with two possible tag answers (A–F).

1 Is San Francisco a very expensive city?
2 Are there many good restaurants there?
3 Did you have a good time there?
4 Would you like to live there?
5 Have you been to Los Angeles, as well?
6 Were you there for very long?

A Yes, there are./No, there aren't.
B Yes, I was./No, I wasn't.
C Yes, it is./No, it isn't.
D Yes, I have./No, I haven't.
E Yes, I would./No, I wouldn't.
F Yes, I did./No, I didn't.

B 'TAG' QUESTIONS

1 **You're lying, aren't you?**
2 **You aren't telling the truth, are you?**

One of the many uses of questions like this is to suggest what you think the answer is. Ken Ishihara believes that the answer to question 1 is 'Yes' and that the answer to question 2 is 'No'. He also asks the following questions:

3 **You already knew he was dead, didn't you?**
4 **You were there when he was killed, weren't you?**

Ken Ishihara believes that the answer to both these questions is 'Yes'.

EXERCISE 31B (ANSWERS OPPOSITE)

Which answer, 'Yes' or 'No', do you think Ken Ishihara believes are true in the following questions?

1 You *don't expect* us to believe you, *do you?*
2 You *paid* the man who killed your lover, *didn't you?*
3 Everything you've told the court *is a lie, isn't it?*
4 You *haven't told* us the truth, *have you?*
5 You *know* the name of Bondy's killer, *don't you?*
6 You *have* told this court lies after lies, *haven't you?*

ANSWERS TO EXERCISES

Ex 1   tick sentences: 1, 4, 5, 7, 8

Ex 2   1 rained   2 went   3 had rained   4 came/was shining   5 started/was going   6 finished/went   7 got/had

Ex 3   1F   2E   3D   4C   5A   6B

Ex 4   1 since   2 for   3 ago   4 on   5 in   6 at

Ex 5   1D   2G   3J   4H   5E   6B   7A   8I   9F   10C

Ex 6   1 if I sit   2 if I looked at   3 you bought   4 it cost   5 why you want   6 you are asking me all

Ex 7   1D   2F   3H   4G   5A   6C   7E   8B

Ex 8   1B   2A/B   3B   4A/B   5A   6A/B   7A/B   8B

Ex 9   1A/B   2B/C   3A   4A/B/C   5A/B/C   6A/C   7B

Ex 10   1G   2D   3A   4E   5H   6C   7F   8B

Ex 11A   1 which   2 who   3 which   4 which   5 which   6 which   7 who   8 which

Ex 11B   sentences 1, 2, 4, 5, 6, 7

Ex 12A   unnecessary words: 4 that   5 that   7 that   9 that

Ex 12B   1 no   2 yes   3 yes   4 no   5 yes   6 yes   7 yes   8 yes   9 no

Ex 13   1B   2C   3C   4A   5B   6B   7C   8A

Ex 14   1A   2B   3B   4A   5B   6A   7A   8B   9B

Ex 15   1B   2E   3C   4A   5D   6F   7A   8E

Ex 16   1 had   2 were   3 were   4 knew   5 saw   6 lived   7 were

Ex 17   1 rains   2 doesn't come   3 were   4 would like   5 had   6 were   7 are   8 stopped

Ex 18   1B   2A   3B   4A   5B   6B   7A   8A

Ex 19   1 can   2 could   3 could   4 Can/Could   5 Can/Could   6 can   7 could   8 can/could   9 could

Ex 20   1E   2C   3G   4B   5A   6F   7D   8H

Ex 21   1D   2B   3E   4A   5C

Ex 22   1B   2B   3B   4A   5A   6A   7B

Ex 23   1D   2C   3B   4A   5A   6F   7E   8B

Ex 24   1 doing   2 to do   3 smoking   4 istening   5 to make   6 closing   7 making   8 to spend   9 to stay   10 reading   11 to read/reading   12 to get up/getting up

Ex 25   1F   2E   3B   4A   5H   6G   7C   8D

Ex 26   1 have/had   2 would/had   3 be/known   4 would/have   5 had won

Ex 27   1 have/cut   2 have/cut   3 going/cleaned   4 had/serviced (mended, repaired)   5 have/built   6 have/done   7 have/delivered   8 have/made

Ex 28   1A   2D   3B   4A   5A   6B   7D   8B

Ex 29   1 asked/to come   2 told/to come   3 asked/to tell   4 told/to tell

Ex 30   1D   2F   3A   4C   5E   6B

Ex 31A   1C   2A   3F   4E   5D   6B

Ex 31B   1 no   2 yes   3 yes   4 no   5 yes   6 yes